Y0-CRQ-405

Legal Almanac Series No. 49

ANIMAL RIGHTS AND THE LAW

by **DANIEL S. MORETTI**

General Editor
Irving J. Sloan

1984
Oceana Publications, Inc.
London • Rome • New York

ACKNOWLEDGMENT

The author gratefully acknowledges the help of Kevin Egan, Jamie Archer, Frank Bajak, Steve Chananie, Max and Gertrude Moretti, Clarence and Carol Weinmann, Nicholas Robinson, and Irving Sloan in writing this book.

The Legal Almanac Series brings you the law on various subjects in non-technical language. These books do not take the place of your attorney's advice, but they can introduce you to your legal rights and responsibilities.

Library of Congress Cataloging in Publication Data

Moretti, Daniel S.
    Animal rights and the law

    (Legal almanac series ; no. 49)
    Bibliography: p.
    Includes index.
    1. Domestic animals—Law and legislation—United States. 2. Animals, Treatment of—Law and legislation—United States. I. Title. II. Series.
KF390.5.A5M67   1984   346.7304'6954   84-2245
ISBN 0-379-11147-0   347.30646954

Manufactured in the United States of America

For my Mother and Father

TABLE OF CONTENTS

PREFACE

Animal law today remains an uneven progression of standards. From a callous acceptance of cockfighting or blind acquiescence in the abuse of beasts of burden, to compassion for stray animals and caring about "humane" slaughter methods, to active measures safeguarding species whose very existence is threatened: society currently enforces laws for each of these moral judgments. The internal inconsistency in values reflects how different public constituencies have educated their legislative bodies at varied points of time.

Animal law is a mixed bag of rules which vary from state to state, and certainly internationally. Nonetheless, some progress can be discerned. For instance, most nations ban whaling today, but those few which insist on killing earth's largest mammals are under increasing pressure, through the International Whaling Commission, to end their practice. Gradually countries are deciding to protect predators such as wolves, rather than to destroy them. Zoological gardens are less jails and more authentic re-creations of the habitats for the animals represented, bred, and studied.

There have been advances during the twentieth century in the ways humans constrain their conduct toward other species. Animal law is the chronicle of how men and women evidence their concern for the welfare of animals. Much remains to be done in educating law-makers who have yet to reform their laws and to enforce the laws now in place. Poaching, for instance, is still a crime actively committed in most states and nations; each year, game wardens bravely defending their society's decision to protect animals, are killed by poachers.

Before the human species learns to live in a more symbiotic relationship with animals, and before animal law can become more effective, substantially more education about animals is needed. Those individuals who care about animals need to know the current state of the law in their region and what it should be.

This handbook provides a ready orientation to the law of animal rights. Although the lawyer may find this text useful to give a summary overview of the principal trends in the laws governing animals, it is the nonlawyer who will find the book to be one of great value. There are very few surveys of animal law available to the public. Dan Moretti and Oceana Publications provide a useful service in writing and in publishing this study.

Those who care about animals will find this book to be a necessary reference. It orients readers to the trends, regressive as well as progressive, in the law. It points to sources for more intensive reading and to the statutes themselves. Most importantly, it documents the next step in law making which a state might take if its legislators cared to advance a more ethical relationship toward animals.

For individuals who wish to better understand the rights accorded animals, this book will be a good introduction.

Nicholas A. Robinson
Deputy Commissioner
and General Counsel
New York State Department of
Environmental Conservation

INTRODUCTION

Although the title indicates that this book is about animal rights, one will soon notice that rights of animals per se are really not discussed. Instead, this book is a compilation of a number of state and federal laws that were enacted to regulate people's actions in regard to animals. One of the major purposes of such legislation is to insure that people will treat animals humanely. For example, people are prohibited from cruelly treating an animal; people are prohibited from inhumanely slaughtering an animal; and people must humanely transport animals.

This book will give an overview of seven areas of animal welfare legislation. They are: anti-cruelty laws, laboratory animal welfare laws, animal trapping laws, animal fighting laws, wildlife legislation, humane slaughter laws and animal transportation laws. Each area is accompanied by a corresponding section in the Appendix. The Appendix will either give the law being discussed or give the reader information as to where the actual law may be found. Since some areas will not be emphasized as much as others, the Appendix will aid those intending further study.

After reading this book, one will realize that there are a number of state and federal laws aimed at protecting animals from mistreatment. Unfortunately, these laws have been largely ineffective. Police officers usually have other things to do besides checking houses to see if pets or other animals are being cruelly treated. State officials are not in the habit of checking cars, trucks, and trains to determine whether animals are being transported under cruel conditions. There are not enough forest officials to make sure traps are checked within the prescribed trap-checking times. Humane societies have neither the money nor the manpower to handle these jobs. In short, lack of enforcement has made many animal welfare laws ineffective. The reader must not forget that although laws and regulations exist, they may not necessarily be as helpful to animals as one might hope. This book should make the reader aware of those animal welfare laws that do exist and, to some extent, how they operate.

Chapter 1
THE ANTI-CRUELTY STATUTES

Until the early part of this century there were few laws to protect animals against cruelty. Animals were only considered to be the property of their respective owners, so, in a sense, animals were no different from other property items like chairs, cars, or trees. Since animals were merely property, their owners could do with them as they pleased. The fact that this often led to starvation, torture, and killing of animals, did not make an impact upon the law.

Today, the law grants animals basic types of protection. One of these protections is that animals should be free from unnecessary inhumane and cruel treatment. All fifty states have now enacted some form of criminal statute prohibiting cruelty to animals. Unfortunately the motivation behind legislation aimed at preventing cruelty to animals is apparently grounded more in an interest in upholding the morals of society than in a sincere interest in animal welfare. Nevertheless, anti-cruelty laws today represent the most substantial legal step toward protecting animals from mistreatment. These laws will be analyzed in this chapter.

What is Cruelty?

Some state laws simply state that no person shall commit cruelty to animals. Others go on to define what is meant by "cruelty." For example, many states expressly prohibit a person from depriving an animal of food, water, or shelter. However, many other states only require that animals be given necessary sustenance. Most states expressly prohibit abandoning an animal, while others only prohibit abandoning a sick or injured animal. Some states actually require that an animal be exercised, others prescribe the minimum dimensions of the cage in which an animal is to be kept. In sum, states seem to concentrate on different aspects of animal welfare. Very few generalizations can be made about today's anti-cruelty laws.

One can say, however, that today's anti-cruelty statutes are broad. By prohibiting anyone from cruelly treating an animal, states prohibit a good deal. Just because certain acts are not expressly prohibited does not mean that they can be committed without fear of violating the law. For example, even if a state does not expressly prohibit cockfighting or dog fighting, promoting such animal fighting may violate a state anti-cruelty law.

The key to determining what sort of act constitutes cruelty in each state depends on several factors. First, how does the law define animal? Second, what kind of activities are expressly or impliedly exempted from cruelty? Third, what level of intent is required for conviction? Fourth, is the punishment imposed for cruelty an effective one? Fifth, is the anti-cruelty law effectively enforced?

What is an Animal?

In prosecuting someone for cruelty to animals, the first issue that must be determined is whether the creature being cruelly treated qualifies as an animal for the purposes of the state's anti-cruelty law. Most states define "animal" to include all living creatures except man. Some, however, do not. States sometimes limit the scope of their anti-cruelty laws by narrowly defining "animal." Some states only protect domestic animals or warm-blooded animals. Other states do not even bother defining "animal."

Exceptions to cruelty

Once it is determined that a cruelly treated creature qualifies as an animal under the state's anti-cruelty statute, it must be determined whether the alleged act of cruelty actually violates the law. Although states have adopted fairly broad language in their anti-cruelty statutes, most have expressly or impliedly exempted certain activities from liability. For example, many states define cruelty as an act, failure to act, or neglect which causes unjustifiable or unnecessary pain to an animal. However, most states have also made hunting, fishing, trapping, slaughtering animals, or experimenting on animals exceptions to their anti-cruelty laws. While there are other laws governing these activities, such activities are, in the eyes of the law, either necessary or justified.

Consequently, the scope of a state's anti-cruelty law is notably restricted by its many exceptions.

Level of Intent—The Qualifying Phrase

Since some degree of intent is almost always required to convict a person of a crime, many states have limited the effect of their anti-cruelty statutes by adopting qualifying phrases requiring a high level of intent. For example, instead of simply convicting any person who, for whatever reason, cruelly mistreats an animal, many states require that cruelty be committed either maliciously, willfully, intentionally, knowingly or recklessly. If a state has not adopted a qualifying phrase such as these, then courts will usually apply one of their own. Each phrase defines a different level of intent. The meanings are given below.

1. <u>Maliciously</u> - One generally acts maliciously if he acts with evil intent.

2. <u>Willfully</u> - One generally acts willfully if he acts intentionally and voluntarily, with specific intent to do something the law forbids.

3.<u>Intentionally</u> - One generally acts intentionally when he desires to cause certain results.

4. <u>Knowingly</u> - One generally acts knowingly when he is aware that his conduct is practically certain to cause a certain result.

5. Recklessly – One generally acts recklessly if he disregards a risk, of which he is aware, that a certain result may occur.

Some of the above levels of culpability are harder to prove than others. For instance, malice and willfullness require the prosecutor to prove the offender committed cruelty to animals with evil intent. In the field of cruelty to animals, the difficulty of proving these levels of culpability often leads to an acquittal. Laws requiring malice or willfullness have been interpreted by some states to convict only the sadistic offender.

Many states however, have adopted the phrase "recklessly." States that permit conviction on a showing that the offender acted "recklessly" have enacted much broader anti-cruelty laws than those requiring malice or willfullness. To prove recklessness, the prosecutor must show that the offender did not exercise due caution in his treatment of an animal.

A few progressive states have actually broadened their anti-cruelty laws to require only a showing that the offender acted with criminal or ordinary negligence. One acts in a criminally negligent manner if he fails to take notice of a substantial risk. In short, he grossly deviates from a reasonable standard of care. Ordinary negligence is established when a person does not act within a reasonable standard of care. The key is that neither criminal negligence nor ordinary negligence requires any degree of intent.

Punishment for Cruelty

The punishment that a state chooses to impose for cruelty to animals reflects its commitment to animal welfare. Almost all states impose varying fines and terms of imprisonment for those committing cruelty to animals. However, since judges have in many instances been reluctant to imprison persons for cruelty to animals, a fine is often imposed. Large fines not only punish offenders but also serve to deter others from committing cruelty in the future. States that impose only small fines for cruelty to animals have clearly limited the effect of their statute, and their commitment to protect animals from mistreatment.

Enforcement

Finally, and perhaps most importantly, it must be pointed out that most anti-cruelty laws are not effectively enforced. Law enforcement officials like police and sheriffs are often more concerned with crimes committed against humans. Very few people who commit cruelty are ever brought into a courtroom and prosecuted. Even if such people were prosecuted, many judges still believe punishing someone for cruelty to animals is ridiculous. While most states have given enforcement powers to ASPCA officials and other humane society agents, these organizations are understaffed. They are often privately funded. Many of their workers are volunteers. In the end, the question of enforcement comes down to money. In light of the small amount of money being spent to enforce anti-cruelty laws, it is obvious that state legislatures have not taken as much of an interest in animal welfare as they might have.

SUMMARIES OF THE ANTI-CRUELTY LAWS
OF THE FIFTY STATES

ALABAMA

Like many other states, Alabama does not define animal. The state's anti-cruelty law is both short and broad. It expressly prohibits any person from intentionally or recklessly subjecting any animal to cruel mistreatment or neglect. The punishment for cruelty to animals is up to six months imprisonment and/or up to $1,000 fine.

ALASKA

Alaska law defines animal to include every vertebrate creature except man and fish. The statute prohibits any person from intentionally inflicting severe and prolonged physical pain upon an animal, or recklessly neglecting an animal whereby severe pain or death is caused. The punishment for either crime is up to one year imprisonment and/or up to a $5000 fine.

ARIZONA

While Arizona law does not expressly define animal, the state's anti-cruelty statute is limited to animals under human control. In other words, the Arizona anti-cruelty statute only protects domestic animals. By limiting cruelty only to domestic animals, the law obviously frees people to do whatever they please to wild animals.

Under the statute, cruelty is committed when a person recklessly subjects an animal or poultry under human custody to cruel mistreatment; or subjects any animal or poultry under his custody to cruel neglect or abandonment. Arizona law punishes cruelty to animals by a maximum of four months imprisonment and/or a fine up to $750.

ARKANSAS

Under Arkansas law, animal is defined to include every living creature. Cruelty to animals takes place when anyone knowingly subjects an animal to cruel mistreatment or neglect. Cruelty is specifically defined as an act or failure to act that results in unjustifiable physical pain or death. In short, the Arkansas law is intended to convict any person who inflicts unjustifiable pain upon an animal and who is aware that he is doing so. The penalty for committing cruelty to animals in Arkansas is a fine up to $1,000 and/or a maximum of one year imprisonment.

CALIFORNIA

California defines animal to include every dumb creature. California has divided its Anti-Cruelty Statute into two sections. The first prohibits any person from maliciously torturing, injuring, or killing an animal belonging to another person. Malice is defined as the intent to do a wrongful act. Torture is defined as any act, or failure to act, that causes unnecessary pain to an animal. In short, the first section prohibits any person from unnecessarily causing pain to an animal belonging to another if that person intended to cause such pain. The penalty for such action is up to one year imprisonment.

The second section is the state's general Anti-Cruelty Statute. It does not require that cruelty be committed to an animal belonging to another. Instead, any animal, including a wild animal, is protected. Generally, the statute prohibits any person from torturing (defined above), or depriving an animal of necessary sustenance, drink, or shelter. The section does not have a qualifying phrase. Consequently, California courts have stated that conviction for torturing an animal requires at least criminal negligence. Courts have also stated that conviction for depriving an animal of food, drink, or shelter requires only ordinary negligence. Cruelty to animals is punishable by six months imprisonment and/or a $500 fine.

COLORADO

Colorado law defines animal to include every living dumb creature. A person commits cruelty to animals when he knowingly, or with criminal negligence, mistreats or neglects an animal. Mistreatment includes every act or failure to act in which unjustifiable pain is caused. Neglect includes the failure to provide any animal with food, water, protection from the elements, exercise, or other proper care for the animal's health.

The penalty for any of the above is a strict one. The maximum sentence of imprisonment is two years. The minimum is six months. The maximum fine is $5,000. The minimum is $500. Colorado's minimum penalty for cruelty to animals is roughly equal to the maximum penalties in most other states.

CONNECTICUT

Animal is defined in Connecticut to include all brute creatures. This definition is generally interpreted to mean any non-human creature. The Connecticut Anti-Cruelty Statute consists of language common to most anti-cruelty laws, but does not restrict such language with qualifying phrases. The law prohibits anyone from overdriving, overworking, torturing, depriving of necessary sustenance, cruelly beating, or unjustifiably injuring any animal. Furthermore, the law requires animals to be given proper food, drink, and shelter. It also prohibits anyone from abandoning an animal in his custody. Perpetration of any of the above acts is punishable by a maximum of one year imprisonment and/or a $250 fine.

Interestingly, Connecticut is one of very few states that require any motorist who hits a dog to "immediately" stop and report the accident to the dog's owner or the police.

DELAWARE

Delaware is one of many states that does not define animal. Cruelty to animals is established when anyone either intentionally or recklessly subjects an animal to cruel mistreatment or cruel neglect. The law defines "cruel mistreatment" as any treatment of an animal that causes unjustifiable pain. Cruel neglect is committed when an animal suffers because the person responsible for the animal has abandoned it or failed to give it proper food, water, shelter, or proper veterinary care. Cruelty to animals is punishable by a maximum of two years imprisonment, and/or a $1,000 fine.

DISTRICT OF COLUMBIA

Animal is defined to include all living and sentient creatures except human beings. Cruelty to animals is broadly defined, without qualifying phrases, to encompass overworking, torturing, tormenting, or cruelly beating any animal. The law also makes it illegal for anyone to fail to

11

provide an animal with proper food, drink, and shelter. The penalty for cruelty to animals in the District of Columbia is a maximum of one year imprisonment and/or a $2,500 fine.

It is also illegal to cruelly abandon any animal. The qualifying word "cruelly" is generally interpreted to mean the unnecessary infliction of pain and suffering. In other words, an animal may be abandoned by its owner if provisions have been made for the animal's well-being. The law however, prohibits abandoning a sick or injured animal whether it is done cruelly or not. Interestingly, the law requires that sick or injured animals do not go without food or water for more than five hours.

FLORIDA

Florida law defines animal as any living dumb creature. In Florida it is illegal to unnecessarily overload, overdrive, torture, torment, beat, or kill any animal. The statute expressly states that the words "torture," "torment," and "cruelty" include every act or omission to act that causes an animal unnecessary pain. It is also illegal to unnecessarily deprive an animal of food, water, or shelter. Cruelty to animals is punishable by a maximum of one year imprisonment and/or a $5,000 fine.

Florida law is somewhat unique in its treatment of confined animals. Not only does it prohibit confining an animal without food or water, but also without exercise. Today, animal exercise is only required in a small number of states.

GEORGIA

Georgia law does not define animal. Under the law, cruelty is established when one's act, failure to act, or neglect causes unjustifiable pain or death to any animal. The penalty for committing cruelty to animals is a maximum of one year imprisonment and/or a $1,000 fine. Although the statute contains no qualifying phrases, courts have generally required that cruelty be committed with malice. Malice is the highest level of culpability used in state anti-cruelty laws. In jurisdictions like Georgia that require malice, it is often only the sadistic offender who will be convicted.

HAWAII

Hawaii defines animal to include every living creature. One commits cruelty to animals if one knowingly or recklessly overdrives, tortures, cruelly beats, or needlessly kills any animal or deprives any animal of necessary sustenance. The words "cruelty" and "torture" are expressly defined to include any act, failure to act, or neglect that causes an animal unjustifiable pain or death. Cruelty to animals is punishable by a maximum of one year imprisonment and/or a $1,000 fine.

IDAHO

Idaho, like many other states, defines animal to include every dumb creature. The Idaho Anti-Cruelty Statute incorporates standard anti-cruelty language without qualifying phrases. The law prohibits anyone from overworking, overdriving, torturing, or subjecting any animal to needless suffering. Cruelty is established when any animal is deprived of necessary sustenance or shelter. Abandoning any animal in a public place also constitutes cruelty. The penalty for cruelty to animals is a maximum of six months imprisonment and/or a fine up to $1000.

ILLINOIS

Illinois law defines animal to include every living creature except man. The Illinois Anti-Cruelty Statute incorporates standard anti-cruelty language without the use of qualifying phrases. The law states that no person may beat, cruelly treat, torment, overload, overwork, or otherwise abuse any animal. The law also expressly prohibits the abandoning of any animal where it may suffer injury, hunger, or exposure.

An owner's duties to his animals are listed by statute. Each owner must provide:

(a) Sufficient quantity of good quality food and water;
(b) Adequate shelter and protection from

14

weather;

(c) Veterinary care when needed to prevent suffering; and

(d) Humane care and treatment.

Violation of any of the above is punishable by a maximum of 30 days imprisonment and/or $500 fine.

INDIANA

The Indiana Anti-Cruelty Statute only protects vertebrate animals in the custody of the offender. In other words, a wild animal, or any animal in the custody of another person would not be protected. Cruelty to animals is established if a person knowingly or intentionally abandons, neglects or cruelly treats an animal in his custody. The penalty is up to 180 days imprisonment and/or a $1,000 fine.

IOWA

Iowa law does not expressly define animal. Unlike most states, Iowa has divided cruelty to animals into two different statutes. The first is called "Injury to Animals." The crime of "Injury to Animals" is committed when any person maliciously kills, disfigures, or poisons any animal belonging to another. Conviction of cruelty would result in a maximum punishment of two years imprisonment and/or a $5,000 fine.

The second offense is simply entitled "Cruelty to Animals." This offense is committed when anyone either intentionally or negligently causes unjustifiable pain or distress to a domestic animal. Cruelty to animals is also committed when one fails to supply a domestic animal with sufficient food and water. To do so would result in a maximum of 30 days imprisonment and/or a $100 fine.

The first law is limited because it requires that the injury be done to an animal belonging to another, and that it be done maliciously. The second law is limited because it only applies to domestic animals. Today, under Iowa law, a person can cruelly treat a wild animal and not be held liable. However, Iowa is one of very few states that penalize mere negligence. In other words, to convict someone of "cruelty to animals," no intent need be proved. All that is necessary for conviction is that the offender deviated from a reasonable standard of care.

KANSAS

Kansas law defines animal to include every living vertebrate except human beings. Cruelty to animals is committed when any person:
(a) Intentionally kills, injures, maims, tortures or mutilates any animal; or
(b) Abandons or leaves any animal in place without making provisions for its proper care; or
(c) Having physical custody of any animal, fails to provide food, water, shelter, opportunity for exercise, and other care needed for the health and well-being of the

animal.

The penalty for committing cruelty to animals is a fine up to $1,000 and/or up to six months imprisonment.

Kansas is one of the few states that expressly require animals to be exercised. Most states simply require food, water, and shelter. Many still do not require shelter.

KENTUCKY

Kentucky law originally defined animal to include every warm-blooded living creature except a human being. Although this same definition is no longer expressly stated in the law, it is apparent that it still would apply since no new language has been used.

A person is guilty of cruelty to animals in Kentucky when he intentionally or wantonly subjects any animal to cruel mistreatment. Cruel mistreatment is established when an animal is beaten, tortured, abandoned, or not provided with adequate food, water, space, and health care. The penalty for cruelty to animals is a fine up to $500 and/or 12 months imprisonment.

LOUISIANA

Despite the fact that Louisiana law nowhere defines animal, the state has enacted a fairly comprehensive Anti-Cruelty Statute. Cruelty to animals is established when any person intentionally or with criminal negligence commits any of the following:

(1) Overdrives, overloads, or overworks an animal.
(2) Tortures, cruelly beats, or unjustifiably injures an animal.
(3) Unjustifiably fails to provide an animal with proper food, drink, shelter, and health care.
(4) Abandons any animal.
(5) Impounds or confines an animal and fails to supply it with proper food, drink, and shelter.
(6) Carries a living animal in or upon a vehicle in a cruel or inhumane manner.
(7) Mistreats any living animal by any act whereby unjustifiable pain or death is caused.

The penalty for committing cruelty to animals is a fine up to $1,000 and/or up to six months imprisonment.

MAINE

Maine law defines animal to include every living sentient creature. A person is guilty of cruelty to animals in Maine if he intentionally, knowingly, or recklessly:

(a) Kills an animal belonging to another without the other's consent; or
(b) Overworks, tortures, poisons, or

abandons an animal he possesses; or

(c)   Deprives any animal he possesses of necessary sustenance, shelter, and proper medical care.

The penalty for cruelty to animals is up to 12 months imprisonment and/or up to a $500.00 fine.

MARYLAND

Maryland law defines animal to include any living creature except man. Cruelty to animals is established when any person:

(1)   Overworks, tortures, or cruelly beats an animal; or

(2)   Inflicts unnecessary suffering upon an animal or unnecessarily fails to provide the animal with nutritious food, water, space, and shelter.

Cruelty to animals is punishable by a maximum fine of $1,000 and/or 90 days imprisonment.

MASSACHUSETTS

While Massachusetts law does not specifically define animal, a Massachusetts court recently stated that goldfish were animals for the purpose of its cruelty laws. Therefore the word animal should be given a broad interpretation.

The Massachusetts Anti-Cruelty Statute incorporates standard anti-cruelty language without qualifying phrases. Basically, cruelty is committed when one overworks, tortures, or treats an animal cruelly. Cruelty is also committed when one unnecessarily fails to provide an animal with proper food, drink, and shelter. Abandoning an animal also constitutes cruelty. The penalty for cruelty to animals is a maximum of one year imprisonment and/or a $500 fine.

Massachusetts Animal Rights Law is exceptional in certain areas. The law expressly forbids anyone from giving away a live animal as a prize or award at any game or contest. Today, very few states have prohibited giving animals away in this manner.

Massachusetts law expressly prohibits any public elementary or high school teacher from allowing the infliction of any pain or injury to any animal in a school experiment. Also, the law prohibits classes from possessing pets unless they can be cared for at all times in a safe and humane nanner.

MICHIGAN

Michigan law defines animal to include all brute creatures. Cruelty is committed when any person overworks, tortures, torments, cruelly beats, or kills an animal. It is also committed when one fails to provide the animal with proper food, drink, and shelter. Cruelty to animals is

punishable by a maximum of three months imprisonment and/or a $100 fine.

MINNESOTA

Minnesota law defines animal to include every living creature except humans. Cruelty to animals is committed in Minnesota when one of the following is established:

(1)   Torture.   No person shall overdrive, overwork, cruelly beat, or unjustifiably injure any animal.

(2)   Nourishment & Shelter.   No person shall deprive any animal of necessary food, water, and shelter.

(3)   Enclosure.   No person shall keep any animal in any enclosure without providing exercise and change of air.

(4)   Abandonment.   No person shall abandon an animal.

(5)   Temporary Abandonment.   No person shall allow any sick animal to lie in any public place for more than three hours after receiving notice.

(6)   Caging.   No person shall cage any animal for public display, unless the cage is constructed to protect the animal from the elements and the horizontal dimensions of the cage are at least four times the length of the animal.

The penalty for violating any of the above is a maximum of 90 days imprisonment and/or a $500 fine.

MISSISSIPPI

Mississippi law defines animal to include every creature except man. Unlike most other states, Mississippi has divided cruelty to animals into two different statutes. The first is the state's standard "Cruelty to Animals" Statute. It prohibits any person from overworking, torturing, unjustifiably injuring or depriving any animal of necessary sustenance. The punishment is up to $500 and/or six months imprisonment.

The second statute is concerned with injury to domestic animals. It prohibits anyone from maliciously injuring or killing any horse, mare, gelding, mule, sheep, cattle, hog, dog, poultry or other livestock. The penalty for such crime is a maximum fine of $1,000 and/or six months imprisonment.

MISSOURI

Like most states, Missouri defines animal to include all creatures except man. The Missouri Anti-Cruelty Statute prohibits any person from willfully and maliciously killing, maiming, wounding, beating, or torturing any animal. The fine imposed for cruelty to animals in Missouri (maximum $55) is one of the lowest in the nation.

MONTANA

Montana law does not define animal. A person commits cruelty to animals in Montana if,

without justification, he knowingly or negligently subjects an animal to mistreatment by:

(a) Overworking, beating, tormenting, injuring, or killing any animal;
(b) Carrying any animal in a cruel manner;
(c) Failing to provide an animal with proper food, drink, or shelter; or,
(d) Abandoning any animal where it may cause injury, hunger, or exposure.

The penalty for cruelty to animals is a maximum of six months imprisonment and/or a $500 fine.

Montana is one of very few states that penalize mere negligence. In other words, no intent or reckless desire to commit cruelty need be proved. All that is necessary for conviction is that the offender deviated from a reasonable standard of care.

NEBRASKA

Nebraska considerably limits the scope of its anti-cruelty statute by defining animal as any domesticated living creature or a wild creature previously domesticated.

Cruelty to animals is committed when any person intentionally or recklessly subjects an animal to cruel mistreatment or neglect, or abandons any animal. The law defines cruel mistreatment as any act or failure to act which causes unnecessary pain to an animal. Cruel neglect is defined as the failure to provide food, water, shelter, health care, and exercise to any animal. Abandoning an animal is defined by law as leaving an animal without making effective provisions for its well-being. Cruelty is punishable by a maximum of six months imprisonment and/or a $1,000 fine.

NEVADA

Nevada law defines animal to include all living creatures except man. A person is guilty of cruelty to animals in Nevada when he:

(1) Overdrives, overloads, tortures, or unjustifiably injures any animal;
(2) Deprives any animal of necessary sustenance such as food and drink;
(3) Willfully engages in any act that causes unjustifiable pain or death to any animal; or
(4) Abandons an animal.

Cruelty to animals is punishable by up to six months imprisonment and/or a $1,000 fine.

NEW HAMPSHIRE

New Hampshire's very comprehensive anti-cruelty statute is only limited by its narrow definition of animal. The law defines animal to include domestic animals or wild animals in captivity. Like many other states, New Hampshire does not protect wild animals.

Cruelty to animals is committed if one:

(a) Negligently deprives an animal of necessary care or shelter;

(b) Negligently beats, cruelly whips, tortures, mutilates, or in any other way mistreats an animal;

(c) Negligently overdrives, overworks, or abuses an animal;

(d) Negligently abandons any animal to be left without adequate care; and

(e) Negligently permits any animal to be subjected to inhumane treatment.

The penalty for cruelty to animals is up to one year imprisonment and/or $1,000 fine.

New Hampshire is one of very few states that penalizes mere negligence. In other words, no intent or reckless desire to commit cruelty need be proved. All that is necessary for conviction is that the offender deviated from a reasonable standard of care.

NEW JERSEY

New Jersey law defines animal to include all brute creatures. Cruelty is committed when any person:

(a) Overdrives, overworks, tortures, torments, deprives of necessary sustenance, unnecessarily or cruelly beats or abuses, or needlessly mutilates or kills a living animal;

(b) Causes such acts to be done; or

(c)   Unnecessarily fails to provide an
animal with proper food, drink, and shelter.

The penalty for cruelty to animals is up to
$250 and/or six months imprisonment.

NEW MEXICO

New Mexico law does not define animal.
Cruelty to animals is divided into two separate
statutes, "Cruelty to Animals" and "Injury to
Animals." "Cruelty to Animals" consists of:

(a)   Torturing, tormenting, depriving of
necessary sustenance, cruelly beating,
mutilating, cruelly killing, or overdriving
any animal;
(b)   Unnecessarily failing to provide any
animal with proper food or drink; or
(c)   Cruelly driving or working any animal
when such animal is unfit for labor.

The penalty for cruelty to animals is up to
six months imprisonment and/or a $500 fine.

"Injury to Animals" is committed when one
willfully and maliciously poisons, kills, or injures
any animal belonging to another.   Injury to
animals is punishable by a maximum of one year
imprisonment and/or a $1,000 fine.

NEW YORK

New York law defines animals to include
every living creature except man. New York's

broad anti-cruelty law uses standard anti-cruelty language without the use of restrictive phrases. Basically, cruelty to animals includes any act, or failure to act, that causes unjustifiable pain, suffering, or death to an animal. Specifically, the statute makes it a misdemeanor for any person to overwork, torture, or deprive any animal of necessary sustenance, food, or drink.

While the statute contains no restrictive phrases, it has been construed to require a culpable state of mind. In People v. O'Rourke, 83 Misc.2d 175 (1975), a New York City Criminal Court judge stated, "[a]lthough the [cruelty] statute does not contain words requiring culpability, unless there is clear legislative intent to impose strict liability, a criminal statute should be construed as requiring mental culpability." In short, conviction of cruelty to animals in New York requires some degree of intent to commit cruelty.

The punishment for cruelty to animals is up to one year imprisonment and/or a $500 fine.

NORTH CAROLINA

North Carolina law defines animal to include any useful creature. The North Carolina Anti-Cruelty Statute basically punishes anyone who willfully, by action or inaction, causes unjustifiable pain, suffering, or death to an animal. The penalty for cruelty to animals is up to six months imprisonment and/or a $500 fine.

The statute is restricted in two ways. First, animal is narrowly defined to include only useful animals. While most domestic animals might be considered "useful," it is obvious that most wild animals would not. Second, the statute requires that cruelty be committed willfully. Willfullness, as defined in the beginning of this chapter, requires evil intent. Like malice, willfullness is difficult to prove.

NORTH DAKOTA

North Dakota law defines animal to include every living animal except humans. The law uses effective language without qualifying phrases. Generally, cruelty includes every act, or failure to act, whereby unnecessary or unjustifiable pain, suffering, or death is caused to an animal. It is illegal for anyone to deprive an animal of food, water, or shelter. Confined animals must be exercised. Abandoning an animal is also prohibited. Caged animals must be protected from the elements and given adequate space. The punishment for violation of any of the above is up to one year imprisonment and/or a $1,000 fine.

OHIO

Ohio law does not define animal. The Ohio Anti-Cruelty Statute incorporates standard language without qualifying phrases. Cruelty is committed when one overworks, overdrives, overloads, or tortures an animal. It is also committed when one deprives an animal of necessary sustenance. Food and water are expressly required only for confined animals. The statute makes no mention of either abandoning an animal or giving it adequate shelter. However, it is arguable that failure to provide an animal with such necessities would be prohibited under standard language of the anti-cruelty law. Conviction of cruelty to animals carries with it a fine up to $200 and/or imprisonment up to 90 days.

Ohio, like several other states, also has enacted a statute aimed specifically at injuring domestic animals belonging to another. Conviction for injuring animals belonging to another requires that the crime be committed either willfully or maliciously.

OKLAHOMA

Animal is defined in Oklahoma as any animal in subjugation or captivity whether wild or tame. Cruelty is committed when any person willfully or maliciously overworks, tortures, kills or cruelly beats or injures any animal. It is also committed when one fails to provide an animal with necessary food, drink, and shelter. The penalty for such action is a maximum of one year imprisonment or up to a $500 fine.

The Oklahoma statute is restrictive in two aspects. First, it has a narrow definition of animal. Apparently wild animals not in captivity would not be protected from any cruelty whatsoever. Second, conviction under the law requires intent. While many states today also require intent, it is often the reckless or negligent offender who causes the most harm. Under Oklahoma law he will not be liable.

OREGON

Oregon law defines animal to include any mammal, bird, reptile, or amphibian. Oregon has enacted a broad anti-cruelty statute without restrictive phrases. Generally, the law strictly prohibits any type of cruel mistreatment or neglect. The penalty for cruelty to animals is a maximum fine of $1,000 and/or imprisonment for up to six months. While the law lacks provisions for shelter for animals, it does expressly state that no animal shall go without food and water for more than 36 hours.

PENNSYLVANIA

Cruelty to animals is also established when one wantonly or cruelly abandons an animal or deprives the animal of food, drink, or shelter. The qualifying words "wantonly" and "cruelly" both connote recklessness. In other words, to be convicted of cruelty in Pennsylvania it must be shown that the offender did not exercise due caution in his treatment of the animal. The penalty for conviction of cruelty to animals is a fine up to $300 and/or up to 90 days imprisonment.

Pennsylvania has adopted a much more severe punishment for injuring an animal belonging to another. A person will be convicted for this crime if he willfully or maliciously maims or disfigures the domestic animal of another person. The penalty for such crime is a fine up to $5,000 and/or up to two years imprisonment. Like many other states, Pennsylvania emphasizes its protection of animals owned or possessed by people rather than wild animals.

RHODE ISLAND

Rhode Island defines animal to include all creatures except human beings. Rhode Island has established a fairly comprehensive anti-cruelty law. It has been divided into three sections. The first section prohibits any person from overworking, torturing, tormenting, or cruelly beating or killing any animal. The law also prohibits anyone from depriving an animal of proper food, drink, or shelter. Conviction of any of the above carries with it a maximum fine of $500 and/or 11 months imprisonment.

The second section prohibits any owner or possessor of an animal from abandoning his animal, or transporting it in a cruel manner. This section carries with it the same punishment as the first section.

The third section prohibits any person from maliciously wounding, killing, or poisoning any animal. If it can be proved that the offender acted maliciously, i.e., with intent to do the wrongful act, then the punishment could be up to

$1,000 and/or two years imprisonment.

SOUTH CAROLINA

South Carolina law defines animal to include all brute creatures. South Carolina has adopted standard anti-cruelty language without qualifying phrases. The law convicts any person who overworks, tortures, cruelly kills, mistreats, deprives of necessary sustenance or shelter, or inflicts unnecessary pain upon any animal. The law also prohibits any owner or possessor of an animal from cruelly abandoning or carrying the animal in a cruel manner. The penalty for violating any of the above is not as great as that required by most other states. The maximum fine is only $100 and the maximum sentence is only 30 days.

SOUTH DAKOTA

South Dakota law defines animal to include every living dumb creature. The South Dakota Anti-Cruelty law states that no person shall overdrive, overload, overwork, torture, torment, deprive of necessary sustenance, drink, or shelter, cruelly beat, mutilate, or cruelly kill any animal. "Torture" and "torment" are defined by law to include any act, or failure to act, whereby unnecessary or unjustifiable pain or suffering is caused. The penalty for cruelty to animals is a maximum of 30 days imprisonment and/or a $100 fine.

Although the South Dakota law applies a

rather weak penalty, it is broader than most other anti-cruelty laws. Generally, the law prohibits anyone from inflicting pain upon any animal. There are no qualifying phrases used in the statute.

TENNESSEE

Tennessee defines animal to include every living creature. Tennessee law broadly defines cruelty without qualifying phrases, to include every act, failure to act, or neglect whereby unjustifiable pain or death is caused to an animal. Like many other states Tennessee prohibits anyone from overdriving, overloading, torturing, tormenting, depriving of necessary sustenance, cruelly beating or killing any animal. Cruelty to animals is punishable by a maximum fine of $1,000 and/or one year imprisonment.

Tennessee, like several other states, has adopted the separate offense of injury to animals. The law prohibits anyone from willfully, wantonly, and knowingly killing, injuring, or poisoning a domestic animal belonging to another. Conviction under this section would not only result in the same fine and imprisonment as mentioned above, but would also include reimbursement for the value of the damage done to the animal.

TEXAS

Texas law defines animal as any domesticated living creature or wild animal living in captivity. Cruelty to animals is committed in Texas when one intentionally or knowingly:

(1) Tortures or seriously overworks an animal.
(2) Fails unreasonably to provide necessary food, care, or shelter for an animal in his custody.
(3) Abandons unreasonably an animal in his custody.
(4) Transports or confines an animal in a cruel manner; or
(5) Kills, injures, or administers poison to an animal belonging to another, without authority or the owner's effective consent.

Conviction for cruelty to animals may result in a maximum fine of $2,000 and/or up to one year imprisonment.

The Texas law, like many other state laws, is restrictive in two areas. First, the law narrowly defines animal. The definition used above does not encompass wild animals. Consequently such animals are not effectively protected from cruelty. Second, the statute requires intent or knowledge. To be convicted of cruelty to animals, it must be shown that the offender was either aware that he was committing cruelty or that he desired to commit cruelty.

UTAH

Utah law does not define animal. Like Texas, Utah law establishes cruelty to animals when one knowingly or intentionally:

(a) Tortures or seriously overworks an animal; or

(b) Abandons an animal in his custody; or

(c) Fails to provide necessary food, care, or shelter for an animal in his custody; or

(d) Transports or confines an animal in a cruel manner; or

(e) Kills, injures, or poisons an animal without legal privilege.

Cruelty to animals is punishable by up to six months imprisonment and/or a $299 fine.

VERMONT

Vermont law defines animal to include all brute creatures. A person commits cruelty to animals in Vermont when he overdrives, overworks, tortures, torments, deprives of necessary sustenance, cruelly beats, or cruelly kills any animal. Cruelty to animals is also established when one having possession of an animal unnecessarily fails to provide it with proper food, drink, and shelter. Abandoning an animal also constitutes cruelty. Any of the above offenses is punishable by a maximum of one year imprisonment and/or $200 fine.

The Vermont Anti-Cruelty Statute uses standard anti-cruelty language without restricting such language with qualifying phrases. The definition of animal is also broad enough to encompass wild animals.

VIRGINIA

Virginia law does not define animal. Cruelty to animals is committed in Virginia when any person overdrives, tortures, ill-treats, abandons, cruelly or unnecessarily beats or kills any animal. Cruelty to animals is also committed when any person deprives an animal of necessary sustenance, food, drink, or shelter. Cruelty to animals is punishable by up to one year imprisonment and/or a $1,000 fine.

WASHINGTON

Washington law defines animal to include all living creatures except man. Washington has enacted a broad anti-cruelty statute. It prohibits any person from cruelly overworking, torturing, tormenting, depriving of necessary sustenance, beating, or killing any animal. The law requires that animals be given proper food, water, shelter, light, and space. Abandoning any animal also constitutes cruelty. Cruelty to animals is punishable by up to 60 days imprisonment and/or $150 fine.

While the statute does not apply a very strict punishment, it is broad in scope. This is because it only uses the qualifying word "cruelly." This term is broadly interpreted to encompass every act, or failure to act, that causes unjustifiable pain to an animal.

WEST VIRGINIA

West Virginia law has defined animal to include domestic animals only. Cruelty to animals is committed when any person cruelly, unnecessarily or needlessly beats, overworks, tortures, or kills an animal. It is illegal to deprive an animal of food or water. Abandoning a sick or injured animal to die is also prohibited. The penalty for cruelty to animals is up to a $100 fine and/or up to six months imprisonment.

The West Virginia Anti-Cruelty Statute is limited in a number of ways. First, animal is narrowly defined to encompass only domestic animals. Second, there is no requirement of shelter for an animal. Third, the statute appears to allow one to abandon an animal as long as the animal is not sick. Finally, the law does not impose a very severe penalty. Since most judges are reluctant to send a person to jail for cruelty to animals, it is often the fine that is used for punishment. Here, the $100 fine does not seem to be an effective punishment or deterrent.

WISCONSIN

While Wisconsin law defines animal to include every living warm-blooded creature except a human being, the Wisconsin Anti-Cruelty Statute states that "no person may treat an animal, whether belonging to himself or another, in a cruel manner." Apparently the anti-cruelty section would not apply to wild animals. Wisconsin law requires persons responsible for an animal to provide the animal with sufficient food and water to maintain the animal's health. The law further requires animals to be given access to shelter from both sunlight and inclement weather. Abandoning any animal is expressly prohibited. The punishment for cruelty to animals is a fine up to $500 and/or up to 30 days imprisonment.

WYOMING

Wyoming law defines animal to include every living dumb creature. Cruelty to animals is committed when a person willfully and maliciously tortures, deprives of necessary sustenance, unnecessarily or cruelly beats or kills an animal. "Torture" is defined by law to include every act or failure to act whereby pain is caused and allowed to continue where there is a reasonble remedy. The penalty for cruelty to animals is a fine up to $100 and/or imprisonment up to one year.

Wyoming, like many other states, restricts the scope of its anti-cruelty law by requiring willfullness or maliciousness. Evil intent to commit the act is an element of both terms. The statute does not penalize the reckless offender. Furthermore, the effect of the statute is limited by the light fine imposed as punishment. Since many judges are reluctant to imprison people for committing cruelty to animals, a fine is often imposed. In contrast to many states, Wyoming's fine is a small one.

Chapter 2
EXCEPTIONS TO THE ANTI-CRUELTY STATUTES

A. LABORATORY ANIMALS

Animal experimentation is an area of animal rights law where state anti-cruelty laws have been generally held to be inapplicable. State laws regulating this experimentation are virtually nonexistent. The reason is the widespread belief that animal experimentation will help improve the physical and psychological condition of humans. As long as these ends are sought, many insist that any degree of animal suffering is justified. Proponents of animal experimentation point to the many breakthroughs in medicine that have resulted from the use of test animals.

Despite the claimed benefits, critics have raised many valid arguments. These critics do not demand the total abolition of animal experimentation; instead, they seek to protect animals from unnecessary suffering. Writers have described numerous instances where laboratory experiments on animals were pointless. Critics have argued that a particular experiment may be unnecessary because it had been already performed by other researchers. Consequently, many experiments may take place for no reason other than to satisfy the whim of a researcher. Criticism has also been directed at researchers who use more animals in an experiment than are actually necessary.

Furthermore, many argue that today there are instruments capable of obtaining the same information as that sought through the use of animals.

THE ANIMAL WELFARE ACT

Since 1880 animal welfare supporters have sought to protect laboratory animals through the enactment of federal legislation. Over the years, more people have become aware of the high degree of suffering that animals often undergo before, during, and after experimentation. More recently, criticism of experimentation practices that are either unnecessary or too broad has led to a public outcry. As a result of this pressure, Congress passed the Laboratory Animal Welfare Act of 1966. The act was amended in 1970 and 1976 to become the Animal Welfare Act (AWA).

As it stands today, the AWA represents a compromise between the claimed needs of laboratory researchers and the demands of animal welfare groups. The act basically seeks to protect animals both before and after an experiment. Unfortunately, however, it affords little protection to animals during an experiment. Consequently, critics continue to denounce the law as having failed to achieve its primary objective of relieving animals from unnecessary suffering during experimentation.

PROVISIONS

According to the Congressional Statement of Policy 7 U.S.C. §2131 (1976), the AWA was enacted to serve three purposes:

(1)   To insure that animals intended for use in research facilities or for exhibition purposes or for use as pets receive humane care and treatment.
(2)   To assure the humane treatment of animals during transportation in commerce; and
(3)   To protect the owners of animals from the theft of their animals by preventing the sale or use of animals which have been stolen.

To meet these objectives, Congress enacted twenty-four provisions which fall into two basic categories: record keeping requirements and licensing standards.

First, the AWA requires that researchers, exhibitors, and carriers of animals keep records. This provision was enacted in an effort to protect owners of animals, and to prevent stolen animals from being used in experiments. The provision specifically requires animal handlers to keep records regarding purchase, sale, transportation, identification, and previous ownership of animals. Research facilities are only required to keep such records regarding dogs and cats.

Second, the law requires that all animal dealers, exhibitors, carriers, and research facilities be licensed. A license will not be issued unless the applicant's facilities comply with the humane standards set forth in the law. Such standards include:

1. Humane housing and handling;
2. Adequate food, water, and shelter;
3. Proper sanitation and ventilation; and
4. Adequate veterinary care, including the proper use of anesthetic or tranquilizing drugs for pain.

Although the above licensing requirements are indeed a great step toward providing safe and humane conditions for animals to be used in experiments, there are no requirements regarding actual experimentation procedure. As a matter of fact the AWA expressly excludes the actual experimentation from any provision of the AWA. The law states:

Nothing in this chapter shall be construed as authorizing the Secretary to promulgate rules, regulations, or orders with regard to design, outlines, guidelines, or performance of actual research or experimentation by a research facility as determined by such research facility.

In short, the law still permits the researcher to do as he pleases. The law makes no attempt to determine whether the objectives sought by the researchers are truly valid and necessary.

Congress, in passing the AWA, has merely assumed that all experiments are justified and, therefore, so is the suffering of the animal. Also, the AWA does not address the most important reason for demanding change: the infliction of unnecessary pain during an experiment.

Section 2143 (c) of the AWA provides for the "appropriate use of anesthetic, analgesic or tranquilizing drugs, when such use would be proper in the opinion of the attending veterinarian of such research facilities." However, if the researcher determines that the objectives of the research project preclude the use of anesthetizing drugs, the experiment may proceed accordingly. Again, the bottom line of the law is noninterference with the researcher.

PENALTIES

Although the AWA does not penalize acts committed during actual experimentation, it does impose rather strict penalties for violations of other provisions. The law states that if the Secretary of Agriculture believes any licensed dealer or exhibitor has violated any provision (i.e., failed to keep records or maintain humane standards), he may have his license revoked. Violators are also subject to a criminal penalty of up to one year imprisonment and/or a $1,000 fine.

Researchers, handlers, and carriers are subject to a fine of up to $1,000 for violating any provisions of the AWA. They are also subject to cease and desist orders if they continue to violate the laws. Finally, any person found to interfere with the enforcement of the act is subject to a fine of up to $5,000 and/or as much as three years imprisonment.

ADMINISTRATION AND ENFORCEMENT

The AWA requires the Secretary of Agriculture to make investigations to ensure that the act is properly enforced. Unfortunately, since 1966, the Department of Agriculture has been reluctant to assume responsibility for the enforcement of the act. At one point, the Secretary of Agriculture went so far as to publicly oppose the 1976 Amendments to the AWA. Today, the AWA is administered by a sub-department of the Department of Agriculture called the Animal and Plant Health Inspection Service (APHIS). Like so many other groups concerned with enforcement of animal welfare laws, this one is also understaffed. It is common for an alleged violator of the AWA to escape a full investigation. Prosecutions are even less common.

CONCLUSION

The AWA's provisions for the licensing of animal dealers and for the marking and identification of animals helps to ensure that laboratory animals are not lost or stolen. More importantly, the AWA requires research

46

facilities to provide animals with certain "minimum requirements" such as food, water, and the appropriate use of anesthetics. Unfortunately, however, the act exempts the actual experiment from regulation. Researchers who subject animals to pain need only fill out annual reports justifying the pain as "necessary" to achieve their scientific objectives.

Finally, the AWA has been poorly administered and enforced. If the AWA is ever to have its full intended effect, the government must make more of a commitment to make the AWA work.

THE SOURCE OF LABORATORY ANIMALS

Few people realize where laboratories obtain many animals for experiments. The answer is "pound seizure." It means the taking of animals from pounds and shelters for the purpose of research and experimentation. This section will examine state pound seizure legislation and will summarize the arguments for and against pound seizure.

STATE IMPOUNDMENT PROCEDURE

Today, virtually every state has enacted statutes directing that unwanted or unclaimed animals, usually cats and dogs, be impounded. The purpose of these laws is to prevent these animals from starving, being hit by cars, or creating nuisances. Once impounded, animals are to be kept for a mandatory holding period —

47

usually three to ten days. If at the end of the mandatory holding period the animal is unclaimed, or its owner cannot be found, the law may direct the pound to do a number of things.

Where there is space available for the animal and funds to provide food, the animal may be held until a home can be found. However, if there is no room or funds, the animal may be humanely destroyed. It is estimated that each year over 10 million dogs are destroyed by public pounds, municipal shelters, and humane societies. Unfortunately, pet overpopulation has gotten so far out of control, that such action is necessary.

POUND SEIZURE

Rather than kill animals outright, most states have authorized pounds and shelters to sell their animals, usually dogs, to licensed research and medical facilities. Indeed, some state laws require that pounds and shelters surrender some or all of their unclaimed or unwanted animals to such facilities. The present Illinois Statute reads in part:

> When so authorized by the appropriate local authority and upon compliance with such reasonable terms relating to expenses incurred by the pound as may be determined by such local authority, supervisors of public pounds operated by or under contract with municipalities or other political subdivisions shall provide from among available

impounded animals 'such number of animals as either a State or Federally licensed institution may request...

Other states have also expressly required shelters and pounds to sell animals to research facilities. They are: Minnesota, South Dakota, Utah, Iowa, Oklahoma, and North Carolina. However, some states have strongly opposed pound seizure and have expressly prohibited it. They are: New Hampshire, Connecticut, New Jersey, Pennsylvania, Rhode Island, Maine, Hawaii, and Massachusetts.

By prohibiting pound seizure, states do not necessarily ensure that research facilities will not receive animals from pounds and shelters. Many research facilities located in states which prohibit pound seizure may simply purchase animals from neighboring states which still permit pound seizure. In December of 1983 Massachusetts not only eliminated pound seizure, but also became the first state to prohibit research facilities from obtaining animals from pounds outside the state. The new law also provides for inspection of research facilities by special police officers of animal protection organizations. The Massachusetts law is by far the most effective anti-pound seizure law to date.

Even if a state does not expressly require that its pounds or shelters deliver their animals to laboratories, they may sell them anyway. Given the choice, many pounds and shelters might sell their animals to laboratories for the money. With the extra money, pounds would be able to take better care of, and find better homes for, the animals they keep. In this respect, only by legally prohibiting pound seizure can states totally eliminate it.

THE CASE FOR POUND SEIZURE

The major benefit to be derived from pound seizure is economic. Since most pounds and shelters sell dogs and cats to research facilities for ten dollars or less, the cost of obtaining animals for experimentation is relatively low. Proponents claim that if pound seizure were eliminated, researchers would have to breed their own animals or pay a professional breeder to do it for them. In either case, proponents have argued, the cost per animal could be as much as 40 times as high. A single university may use as many as 2,000 animals a year. About 200,000 dogs were used in medical experiments in 1980. Obviously the cost of medical and scientific research would increase if pound seizure were eliminated.

Then there is the "die anyway" argument. After pointing to the number of animals destroyed in pounds and shelters, proponents note that since these animals will "die anyway," their lives should not be wasted. Researchers argue if animals were sold to facilities, instead of being destroyed, their lives (and deaths) could help the human race.

THE CASE AGAINST POUND SEIZURE

Critics have stated that the fundamental problem with pound seizure is the type of animal that is seized and ultimately subjected to laboratory conditions. Researchers do not choose unhealthy or unmanageable strays. Instead, they will take those dogs and cats which are healthy, docile, and not sensitized to pain. This selection process strongly suggests that the animals used in experiments were once pets.

Critics also point to those states that have sought to ban pound seizure. New York, for example, recently repealed its Pound Seizure Statute. The New York State Senator who authorized the measure recently stated, "We have received no information that the inability to receive pound animals has in any way affected research to any noticeable degree." If this contention is true, the logical argument advanced by pound seizure proponents loses much of its strength.

Another argument is that pound seizure adds to the animal over population problem. Many people, who can no longer take care of their pets, may be reluctant to take their pets to a pound or shelter for fear it will be sent to a laboratory. Instead, they will simply abandon their animals. These abandoned animals then breed with other animals, the result being an increase in the animal population.

Pound seizure also violates the principle

51

behind animal pounds and shelters. Few people disagree that pounds and shelters were originally created to provide public protection and sanctuary for unwanted or unclaimed animals. Such animals were to be cared for until suitable homes could be located. If no home could be found, they were to be humanely destroyed. Pound seizure has eradicated this humane concept of pounds and shelters.

Critics also argue that selectively bred animals are better suited for experimentation. First there is no emotional problem since these animals, unlike former pets, are not accustomed to love and care. Second, selectively bred animals are better suited for experimentation because their health and genetic backgrounds are already known to a researcher.

CONCLUSION

Basically, the pound seizure issue pits the economic and scientific values of its proponents against the emotional arguments of its critics. The fear of one day seeing one's pet in a laboratory is not easy to accept. However, the vast majority of states today accept it in the name of science.

B. ANIMAL TRAPPING LAWS

Trapping is another area of animal rights law where state anti-cruelty laws have been generally held to be inapplicable. Each year millions of animals are caught in traps. Most are caught for their fur, many are caught because they are considered "nuisance animals." The overwhelming majority of such traps are of the legholding type, i.e., the trap clamps, with tremendous pressure, upon an animal's leg. Although no direct statistics are kept, it is clear that tens of thousands of animals escape capture by gnawing off their trapped leg. Others die within days, even hours, of exposure, starvation, and thirst. Many trapped animals simply die of shock. Some are eaten by predators. When an unwanted animal is mistakenly trapped, as often happens, it usually must be killed because it is too seriously injured to continue on its own. In sum, nobody can deny the extreme suffering caused by trapping.

In addressing the issue of trapping, state legislatures have taken the position that the economic interests of society (e.g., the fur industry) outweigh animal welfare. The few state laws that do exist today are not vigorously enforced. These laws do not necessarily prevent animals from being trapped. If anything, such laws are aimed at alleviating an animal's suffering once it has been trapped. Each state has its own laws and regulations regarding trapping. A selection of some of the broader provisions appear below.

TRAP CHECKING LAWS

Perhaps the most important state laws regarding trapping are those requiring trappers to check their traps at prescribed intervals. By

53

frequently checking his traps, a trapper can prevent protracted animal suffering. As the laws stand today, Montana is the most progressive. Its laws expressly require that traps be checked every 12 hours.

Many states require that traps be checked every 24 hours. They are:

Alabama	Kentucky	New York
Arizona	Louisiana	No. Carolina
Arkansas	Maine	Ohio
California	Maryland	Rhode Island
Connecticut	Massachusetts	Vermont
Georgia	Missouri	Virginia
Indiana	Nebraska	West Virginia
Iowa	New Hampshire	
Kansas	New Jersey	

Several states have required that traps be checked every two, three, or four days. They are:

Mississippi – 36 hrs.	New Mexico – 48 hrs.
Pennsylvania – 36 hrs.	Utah – 72 hrs.
Tennessee – 36 hrs.	Washington – 72 hrs.
Colorado – 48 hrs.	Wyoming – 72 hrs.
Idaho – 48 hrs.	

Some states have no requirement that traps be checked. They are:

Alaska	Iowa	North Dakota
Florida	Michigan	South Dakota
Illinois	Minnesota	Texas
		Wisconsin

LAWS BANNING TEETH TRAPS

The teeth trap causes more suffering than any other type of leghold trap. It not only clamps on an animal's leg, but also bites into it. The following states have prohibited use of teeth traps:

Arkansas	New York
California	North Carolina
Connecticut	Ohio
Massachusetts	Oklahoma
Missouri	Pennsylvania
Rhode Island	

LAWS PROHIBITING TRAPS BEING PLACED TOO CLOSE TO ANIMAL'S DEN

Perhaps in a humane gesture, some states have prohibited the placing of traps too close to an animal's den or hole. They are:

Arkansas	Iowa
Connecticut	Michigan
Idaho	Pennsylvania

There are, of course, other laws and regulations dealing with trapping. States generally require that traps be clearly identified and that trappers be licensed. Other states even require that trappers take a course in trapping before they may be licensed. Many states require that both trappers and fur dealers keep records and submit reports. For a list of selected state trapping laws see Appendix C.

PENALTIES AND ENFORCEMENT

Violation of the "Trapping Laws" is usually punishable as a small misdemeanor or violation accompanied by a fine. Occasionally a state will punish a trapping offender to the same extent that a person is punished for cruelty. (But this is exceptional.) A bigger problem today might not be punishing offenders but finding them. Law enforcement officials are not in the habit of entering forests to make sure a suspect's traps are checked according to the requirements. On the other hand, a more stringent penalty for violators would probably result in fewer violations. As always, the remedy rests with the legislature. So far, their favor has fallen upon the fur shopper rather than the fur bearer.

Chapter 3
LAWS PROHIBITING ANIMAL FIGHTING

Since the beginning of civilization, animal fighting has proven to be a source of great amusement for many people. When one realizes that in early times the pitting of humans against each other as gladiators was widely accepted, it is not difficult to understand that animal fighting still remains a popular attraction in many areas. It is obvious, however, that over the recent years the popularity of animal fighting has significantly declined. Concern for animals has increased to the extent that most people consider animal fighting to be a very cruel activity. Furthermore, most legislators have determined animal fighting to be damaging to public morals. In an effort to put a stop to animal fighting, nearly all states have now enacted laws prohibiting animal fighting. The federal government has also enacted certain laws to prevent animal fighting.

STATE LAWS

Today, dog fighting is prohibited in every state. Unfortunately, however, cockfighting is not expressly prohibited in a handful of states. They are: Arizona, Arkansas, Florida, Kansas, Louisiana, New Mexico, Oklahoma and Virginia. The average state law prohibiting fighting reads something like this:

NEW YORK

Agriculture & Markets Law Section 350.
"Definitions. 1. 'Animal' as used in this
article, includes every living creature
except a human being."

Section 351.   "Keeping a place where
animals are fought. A person who keeps or
uses, or is in any manner connected with,
or interested in the management of, or
receives money for the admission of any
person to, a house, apartment, pit or place
kept or used for baiting an animal or
causing an animal to engage in combat
either with another animal or with a
person, except in exhibitions of a kind
commonly featured at rodeos, and any
owner or occupant of a house, apartment,
pit or place who willfully procures or
permits the same to be used or occupied
for such baiting or combat, is guilty of a
misdemeanor."

Section 352.   "Instigating fights between
animals.   A person who sets on foot,
instigates, promotes, or carries on, or does
any act as assistant, umpire, or principal,
or is a witness of, or in any way aids in or
engages in the furtherance of any fight
between cocks or other birds, or between
dogs, bulls, bears, or other animals, or
between any such animal and a person or
persons, except in exhibitions of a kind

commonly featured at rodeos, premeditated by any person owning, or having custody of such birds or animals, is guilty of a misdemeanor punishable by a fine not less than ten dollars, nor more than one thousand dollars, or by imprisonment not less than ten days nor more than one year, or both."

The former New York Law represents a fairly average law because it punishes the organizer, promoter, and owner of the premises to the same extent that it punishes the spectator. (New York has since amended its law, See Appendix I). Only a minority of states punish those who actually institute the animal fight to a much greater extent than those who only attend it. The goal of such states is to stop animal fighting at its source. Many of these states only punish spectating at an animal fight as a violation accompanied by a small fine. Other states, like Colorado, Iowa, Kentucky, Texas, and Wyoming have no express punishment for the spectator at a cockfight.

Some states that do not have specific provisions regarding animal fighting have held animal fighting to be illegal under the state's anti-cruelty law. Connecticut, Pennsylvania, Hawaii, Kentucky, Maine, Montana, Texas, Utah, and West Virginia, have expressly prohibited animal fighting in their anti-cruelty laws. On the other hand, Arizona, Kansas, New Mexico, and Oklahoma have already determined that cockfighting does not constitute cruelty to animals.

59

FEDERAL LAWS

Abraham Lincoln is reported to have had this response to advocates of federal abolition of cockfighting: "As long as the Almighty permitted intelligent men, created in his image and likeness, to fight in public and kill each other while the world looks on approvingly, it's not for me to deprive chickens of the same privilege." Lincoln would be surprised to learn that the federal government has passed legislation specifically aimed at eliminating animal fighting.

In 1976, the Animal Welfare Act, 7 U.S.C. 2131 (1976), was amended to help put a stop to illegal animal fighting. The law prohibits anyone from moving an animal in interstate commerce to exhibit, sponsor, deliver, or sell that animal for the purpose of fighting. The law also prohibited anyone from using the mails to promote animal fighting. The relevant sections read:

(a)   It shall be unlawful for any person to knowingly sponsor or exhibit an animal in any animal fighting venture to which any animal was moved in interstate or foreign commerce.

(b)   It shall be unlawful for any person to knowingly sell, buy, transport, or deliver to another person or receive from another person for purposes of transportation, in interstate or foreign commerce, any dog or other animal for purposes of having the dog or any animal participate in an animal fighting venture.

(c)   It shall be unlawful for any person to knowingly use the mail service of the United States Postal Service or any interstate instrumentality for purposes of promoting or in any other manner furthering an animal fighting venture except as performed outside the limits of the States of the United States.

(d)   Any person who violates Subsection (a), (b), or (c), shall be fined not more than $5,000 or imprisoned for not more than 1 year, or both, for each such violation.

Subsection (e) makes it clear that these provisions will not apply to cockfighting that will take place in a state where cockfighting is not illegal. Subsection (f) authorizes the Secretary of Agriculture, who is responsible for enforcing the act, to use the assistance of the F.B.I. and other federal law officials to enforce the act.

ENFORCEMENT AND EFFECT

It is difficult to say whether state and federal legislation have effectively helped put a stop to animal fighting. Federal authorities have complained that they do not possess the resources to enforce effectively the animal fighting provisions of the Animal Welfare Act. The Department of Agriculture has stated that such laws are the responsibility of state and local governments. Consequently, critics have argued that the animal fighting provisions are meaningless.

Critics also contend that state laws have not accomplished their objectives of eliminating animal fighting. Many organizers of animal fights have simply moved their operations "underground." In other words, the laws have only served to make animal fighting a private attraction instead of a public one. On the other hand, the laws have had the effect of precluding prospective spectators from attending an animal fight because they never had the opportunity to hear about it. A smaller audience should result in a smaller number of fights. Nevertheless, there is little doubt that animal fighting, especially cockfighting, continues to take place despite such legislation.

Chapter 4
LAWS TO PROTECT WILDLIFE

This chapter will give an overview of both state and federal wildlife legislation. The first section will deal with state wildlife laws. This section will emphasize the policies that shaped state wildlife laws. The second section will deal with federal wildlife laws. It will concentrate on some of the laws that have had a significant effect on our national wildlife.

A. STATE WILDLIFE LAWS

Until the turn of the century there were virtually no state or federal laws to protect wildlife. The laws that did exist were rarely enforced. This condition unfortunately produced some alarming results. A good example of such a result might be near extinction of the American buffalo. Thousands of years ago the buffalo came to America from Asia across what is now the Bering Strait. The buffalo roamed the country in great herds, moving north in the summer and south in the winter. The Indians of the plains lived off the buffalo for many years. Yet it was not until the white man came to hunt buffalo, at the end of the nineteenth century, that the herds started to disappear.

People have estimated that the white man killed between 30 and 90 million buffalo. With crews of trained hunters, they systematically shot buffalo to meet the demand back east and abroad for buffalo products: tongues were considered a delicacy, buffalo hide furniture was then fashionable, the bones were used for fertilizer. Furthermore, a mass slaughter was organized by the United States Army, as part of a plan to starve the Indians. By the turn of the century the number of buffalo in the United States had been reduced to fewer than 1,000.

In addition to buffalo, a number of other animals were also threatened with extinction. By the turn of the century, deer had almost disappeared from the eastern seaboard. Beaver and turkey were similarly threatened. Several species of birds had also virtually disappeared. In short, for various reasons, the buffalo were not alone on their path to extinction.

The cause of most animal underpopulation was based on several factors. First, and most significantly, part of the population still relied on market hunters, i.e., those who hunted animals for their meat and sold it. Second, there were the many sport hunters. Third, there were the many commercial interests, i.e., those who killed for fur, and to eliminate predators. These three groups together were largely responsible for decimating many species of wildlife.

By the beginning of this century a number of state legislators became aware of what was happening to their wildlife. Many decided it was time to take some type of action to save what species they could. States began by creating a number of programs to limit, (1) the number of hunters; (2) the number of animals taken; and (3) the market for such animals. By eliminating, or at least limiting, these incentives to hunt, states believed they could revitalize many species threatened with extinction.

Perhaps the market hunter was the easiest target. Since the market hunter hunted meat for the consumer market, his effect could be diminished by eliminating his market. It so happened that by the early part of this century domestic agricultural production was expanding; consequently, it was not long before the market hunter was no longer needed. Domestic agricultural producers (i.e., cattle ranchers) could supply meat at a cheaper price. By greatly reducing the number of market hunters, states had eliminated one of the primary causes of animal underpopulation.

In order to help limit the number of sport hunters, states devised a licensing system. Many states began to require that a license holder meet certain eligibility requirements, such as age and residence in the state granting the license. While eligibility requirements proved successful in limiting the number of sport hunters, licensing also proved a conserving element in a number of other areas. First, licensing allowed state agencies to determine how many hunters were in the field. Second, since licensing requirements forced hunters to report how many animals they killed, agencies were able to keep track of the number of animals left surviving in a given area. Third, with this information available to them, wildlife officials were able to make accurate decisions regarding future wildlife policy. State licensing requirements not only enabled states to limit the number of hunters, but also allowed them to keep track of the number of animals killed. Therefore the herds could be regulated.

The issue of funding to administer and enforce wildlife regulations presented a problem (and remains a problem) to states wishing to protect their wildlife. Insuring that hunters and fishermen comply with rules regarding time of hunting, number of animals killed, and reporting procedures is not an easy task. Interestingly, states found a funding base in their licensing system. By requiring hunters and fishermen to pay a fee for hunting and fishing licenses, states were able to accumulate the funds necessary to administer and enforce their wildlife programs. Consequently, the achievements made by states to protect and preserve wildlife have been substantially funded by hunters and fishermen.

In the early part of this century states also took an active role in limiting the number of animals taken by hunters. First, states enacted bag limits which generally specify the maximum number of animals that could be taken by a hunter. Second, states limited hunting to certain seasons. Consequently, hunters only had a specified time period in which to hunt. State legislators could shorten or lengthen the season depending on the status of the hunted animal.

Third, states attempted to limit the methods of hunting. Today, for example, many states expressly prohibit using helicopters for hunting purposes. On the other hand, many states encourage people to hunt with bow and arrows instead of guns. The above states' actions have been useful in helping to revitalize the overall number and health of many species.

States have also made other efforts to replace animals in areas where they had once been abundant. "Stocking" — the adding of captive-reared animals to areas already populated by the species in an attempt to raise the population — has largely proved unsuccessful. Studies have shown that previously captured animals cannot stand being reintroduced to the wildlife. In short, many do not survive. On the other hand, transferring native animals has proved successful in increasing area animal populations.

While states have regulated the hunting of most animals, they have purposely failed to protect certain other animals from commercial exploitation. These other animals, because of their abundance and predatory nature, have become the target of a policy called "predator control." The goal of "predator control" is to protect livestock and people from certain predators, usually coyotes, beavers, and foxes. As a result, these predators remain virtually unprotected throughout the United States.

Predators   are   often   controlled   by

something called the bounty system. The bounty system is one of the oldest wildlife management techniques in the world. It is implemented when a state, municipality, or county offers money for the killing of a given predator. For example, Alaska paid bounties for wolves, New Mexico for coyote, and Mississippi for beaver. The system has worked to effectively rid certain areas of certain predators.

Predator control is in the interest of the state, because it protects people, their property, and livestock from interference. The problem with predator control and the bounty system is that it results in the massive slaughter of animals. Earlier in this century many objects of predator control became endangered species. The wolf, for example, is now an endangered species in all states except Alaska. The bobcat and grizzly bear are similarly threatened. Today, both New York and California have prohibited bounties except in extreme circumstances. Nevertheless, states have generally found predator control to be in their interest, and it therefore remains largely unregulated.

On the whole, it is safe to say that most states acted just in time to save a number of species of wildlife from extinction. While the buffalo have gradually returned in a number of areas, other animals, like beaver, deer, and turkey, are evidence of nature's ability to rebound quickly.

B. FEDERAL WILDLIFE LAWS

For many years laws regulating wildlife existed primarily on the state level. More recently however, when faced with the extinction and threatened extinction of a number of species of wildlife, some states refused to take appropriate action. This inaction was largely due to political pressure from hunting and agricultural groups. As a result, the federal government was compelled to take action to protect this nation's wildlife. This section will focus on four federal wildlife protection acts: The Endangered Species Act, The Marine Mammal Protection Act, The Wild and Free-Roaming Horses and Burros Act, and the Migratory Bird Treaty Act. The major emphasis will be put on The Endangered Species Act because of its controversial nature and far-reaching effect.

1. THE ENDANGERED SPECIES ACT

The Endangered Species Act (ESA), 16 USCA 1531, was enacted by Congress in 1973. Over the last ten years the ESA has helped to protect endangered species from extinction. Although the effect of the ESA was notably weakened by amendments in 1978, it still represents a strong national commitment to the preservation of many species of wildlife, fish, and plants.

Prior to 1973, other endangered species protection legislation had not been effective.

The Endangered Species Preservation Act of 1966 basically called for nothing more than the acquisition of land for the protection of certain species. The Endangered Species Conservation Act of 1969 essentially did little more than to create a list of worldwide Endangered Species. In short, the ESA of 1973 was the first effective piece of federal legislation to protect endangered or threatened species.

REASONS FOR THE ESA

By 1973, Congress was well aware that economic growth and development in the United States had already led to the extinction of a number of plants, fish, and wildlife. Many other species were also threatened with extinction. Congress stated that endangered species should be protected because they were of "esthetic, ecological, educational, historical, recreational, and scientific value to the nation and its people."

Although any one of these values would justify the preservation of an endangered species, the most important benefit is the scientific value of any given species. Congress noted in its hearings that each species is a repository of unique information. It is possible that a certain species may possess the information necessary to cure a once incurable disease. If that species were allowed to become extinct, its information would be gone forever.

The Congress also stated that protecting endangered species would be in compliance with a number of international conservation treaties that the United States had signed. Since the United States was a party to several such treaties, it was obligated to enact legislation consistent with their terms.

THE PURPOSE OF THE ESA

In Section 1531 the Congress stated the three major purposes of the ESA. They are:

1. To provide a means whereby the ecosystems upon which endangered species depend may be conserved.
2. To provide a program for the conservation of such endangered and threatened species.
3. To take such steps as may be necessary to achieve the purposes of international conservation treaties which the United States had signed.

The Congress also established the policy considerations that went into determining the ESA's purpose.

HOW TO DETERMINE IF A SPECIES IS ENDANGERED OR THREATENED

Section 1532 defines the terms "endangered species" and "threatened species." An "endangered species" is "any species which is in danger of extinction throughout all or a significant portion of its range." A "threatened species" is "any species which is likely to become an endangered species within the foreseeable future throughout all of a significant portion of its range."

In Section 1533 the Congress further set up guidelines for determining whether a species is endangered or threatened. They are:

1. The present or threatened destruction, modification, or curtailment of the species' habitat or range;
2. The over-utilization of the species for commercial, sporting, scientific, or educational purposes;
3. Disease or predation;
4. Inadequacy of existing regulatory mechanisms; and
5. Other natural or man-made factors affecting its continued existence.

The Secretary of the Interior, who is responsible for enforcing the ESA, is required to use "the best scientific and commercial data available in determining whether a species is endangered or threatened."

THE ENDANGERED SPECIES LIST

The law requires the Secretary of the Interior to publish a list of endangered and threatened species. The list must also specify in what areas the species is endangered or threatened. The secretary is required to review the status of any listed or unlisted species on a petition from an interested person. The person must, however, be able to present substantial evidence that a review is warranted. The secretary is also authorized to list species that are similar to those species already listed as endangered or threatened.

REGULATIONS

Section 1533 (f) of the ESA gives the secretary the authority to promulgate regulations to carry out the purposes of the ESA. Such regulations must be adopted in accordance with standard procedures set forth in U.S. law. However, in emergency circumstances, i.e., those posing significant threats to the well-being of any species, the secretary may issue regulations immediately to provide for the conservation of any listed species. The secretary must also publish detailed reasons why immediate action is necessary. An emergency resolution is effective for 240 days, and may be withdrawn unless scientific evidence exists to support it.

COOPERATION WITH THE STATES

Section 1535 of the ESA authorizes the Secretary of the Interior to enter into cooperative agreements with any state that wishes to implement an "adequate and active program" for the conservation of endangered or threatened species. Whether a state program qualifies as "adequate and active" depends on five factors. The secretary must find:

1. That the State agency has authority to conserve local endangered or threatened species;
2. That the program is consistent with the policies and purposes of the ESA;
3. That the State agency is authorized to commence investigations to determine the status of endangered or threatened species;
4. That the state agency is authorized to establish similar programs;
5. That provisions are made for public participation in designating resident endangered or threatened species or plans are made under which immediate attention will be given to species the State agency or the Secretary agree are threatened or endangered.

Once a program has qualified as "Adequate and Active," the Secretary may enter into a cooperative agreement with the State. The Secretary may also provide financial assistance. Funds are to be distributed based on the following:

1. The readiness of the state to proceed with its program;
2. The number of endangered or threatened species within the state;
3. The potential for success of the program; and
4. The relative urgency of each state's situation. The section also states that the federal share of any state program may not exceed two-thirds of the total cost.

Since 1980, the total federal budget for the state programs has been $12 million per year.

INTER-AGENCY COOPERATION

Section 1536, which establishes the duties of federal agencies under the ESA, is by far the most controversial section of the ESA. Originally the section read:

> The Secretary shall review other programs administered by him and utilize such programs in furtherance of the purposes of this chapter. All other Federal departments and agencies shall, in consultation with and with the assistance of the Secretary, utilize their authorities in furtherance of the purposes of this chapter by carrying out programs for the endangered or threatened species listed pursuant to section 1533 of this title and by taking such action necessary to insure that the actions authorized, funded, or carried out by them do not jeopardize the continued existence of such endangered species which is determined by the Secretary, after consultation as appropriate with the affected States to be critical.

The above section was responsible for stopping a number of federal projects because such projects jeopardized the existence of certain endangered or threatened species. The most famous case arising under this section was Tennessee Valley Authority v. Hill, 437 U.S. 153

(1978).   In that case the Supreme Court held
that because of the existence of the snail darter,
an endangered species, the $120 million Tellico
Dam   Project   in   Tennessee   could   not   be
completed.

Much negative publicity resulted from the
Supreme Court's decision in the Hill case, as well
as several other cases.   In the Hill case, many
people could not understand why a multi-million
dollar project, along with countless jobs, had
been wasted to protect some creature that
nobody had ever heard of.   As criticism of the
law increased, Congress eventually gave in.   In
1978, the section was amended.   Section 1536
now reads:

(2)   Each Federal agency shall, in
consultation with and with the assitance of
the Secretary, insure that any action
authorized, funded, or carried out by such
agency is not likely to jeopardize the
continued existence of any endangered
species or threatened species or result in
the destruction or adverse modification of
habitat of such species which is determined
by the Secretary, after consultation as
appropriate with affected States, to be
critical, unless such agency has been
granted an exemption for such action by
the Committee pursuant to subsection (h)
of this section.   In fulfilling the
requirements of this paragraph each
agency shall use the best scientific and
commercial data available.

The key distinguishing factor between the 1973 section and the 1978 amendment is that the latter establishes an "Endangered Species Committee" which is empowered to grant exemptions to the law. The committee is made up of seven members: the Secretaries of Agriculture, Army, and Interior; the Chairman of the Council of Economic Advisors; the Administrators of the EPA and the National Oceanic and Atmospheric Administration; and one person appointed by the president.

The law states that the committee's determination whether an exemption should be granted is to be based upon the following factors:

A. There are no reasonable or prudent alternatives to the Agency's action;

B. The benefits of the Agency's action clearly outweigh the benefits of alternative courses of action, and such action is in the public interest; and

C. The action is of regional or national significance; and

D. The Agency will take reasonable mitigation and enhancement measures such as "live propagation, transplantation, and habitat acquisition and improvement."

If five of the seven committee members agree that the above factors have been met then the exemption is granted. Furthermore, once an exemption is granted, it remains permanent unless the secretary finds that the exemption would result in the extinction of the species.

In conclusion, it is clear that the once powerful effect of section 1536 was substantially weakened by the 1978 amendments. The 1973 statute had prohibited completely federal projects from interfering with endangered or threatened species. The statute today brings into play the public interest behind the federal project and allows the government to balance it with the foreseeable harm to the threatened or endangered species.

PROHIBITED ACTS

Section 1538 of the ESA prohibits certain acts by citizens of the United States or those subject to its jurisdiction with respect to endangered and threatened species. Specifically, the section makes it illegal for any person to:

(A)   import any such species into, or export any species from the United States;

(B)   take any such species within the United States or the territorial sea of the United States;

(C)   take any such species upon the high seas;

(D)   possess, sell, deliver, carry,

transport, or ship, by any means whatsoever, any such species taken in violation of subparagraphs (B) and (C);

(E)   deliver, receive, carry, transport, or ship in interstate or foreign commerce, by any means whatsoever and in the course of a commercial activity, any such species;

(F)   sell or offer for sale in interstate or foreign commerce any such species; or

(G)   violate any regulation pertaining to such species or to any threatened species of fish or wildlife listed pursuant to section 4 of this Act [16 USC §1533] and promulgated by the Secretary pursuant to authority provided by this Act.

ENFORCEMENT

Interestingly, section 1540 (g)(1) authorizes any person to commence a civil suit in federal district court to enjoin any person who is allegedly in violation of the ESA or its regulations. However, the law provides that no action may be commenced until sixty days after notice of a violation has been given to the Secretary of the Interior.

Section 1540 (a) authorizes the Secretary

of the Treasury to pay up to $2,500 to any person who furnishes information which leads to a finding of civil violation or criminal conviction under any provision of the ESA. Violations of the ESA can result in fines as high as $20,000 and/or up to one year imprisonment.

2. THE MARINE MAMMAL PROTECTION ACT

Like the Endangered Species Act, the Marine Mammal Protection Act (MMPA), 16 USC 1361 (1976), represents a major development in wildlife legislation. The MMPA was enacted in 1972 to protect sea dwelling, warm-blooded, air breathing creatures. This category includes whales, dolphins, porpoises, sea otters, polar bears, seals and walruses. The MMPA was enacted because Congress found a number of such creatures to be in danger of extinction, primarily due to economic exploitation.

PURPOSE

The primary objective of the MMPA is to maintain an "optimum sustainable population keeping in mind the optimum carrying capacity of the habitat." The act defines this population level as:

> The number of animals which will result in the maximum productivity of the population of the species, keeping in mind the carrying capacity of the habitat and the health of the ecosystem of which they form a constituent element.

PROVISIONS

To carry out its primary objective, the MMPA places a moratorium on the taking or importing of any marine mammals or marine mammal products. However, the statute also provides for a number of exceptions to the moratorium. These include: (1) Certain marine mammals that may be taken for scientific research or public display. (2) Alaskan natives who are dependent upon certain marine mammals for survival. (3) Other groups who also require marine mammals to survive may receive a hardship exemption.

However, the most controversial exception involves the incidental killing and injuring of dolphins and porpoises by tuna fishermen. For many years, tuna fishermen have relied on schools of dolphins and porpoises to locate tuna. In the process of netting the tuna, many dolphins and porpoises are killed or injured. Congress was forced to balance the interest of the tuna industry with that of the need to preserve and protect dolphins and porpoises. Section 1371 (a)(2) of The MMPA represents a compromise between those two interests.

The goal of section 1371 (a)(2) is to reduce the injury and mortality rate of dolphins and porpoises "to insignificant levels approaching zero." To achieve this goal, the section requires that tuna fishermen use the best marine mammal safety equipment practicable. The Secretary of the Interior is authorized to set forth standards on the number of dolphins and porpoises permitted to be taken incidentally to tuna fishing. Any country whose fishing practices result in the killing and injuring of dolphins and porpoises in excess of such standards will be prohibited from exporting their fish or fish products into the United States. Today, as a result of such legislation, the number of dolphins and porpoises killed or injured has been reduced.

The MMPA also exempts any activity covered by an existing international treaty. For example, Pacific fur seals are hunted by the United States pursuant to a 1957 treaty signed by the U.S., Canada, and Japan. This hunting does not violate the MMPA because it is done in accordance with the treaty. On the other hand, the MMPA expressly prohibits the importation of any Seal young, pregnant, or inhumanely taken. Since no treaty covers this type of hunting, the importation of "clubed-to-death" baby harp seals from Canada is prohibited.

The MMPA also gives the Secretary of the Interior the power to exempt any species of marine mammal from the MMPA if he finds, on the basis of the best scientific evidence available, that the taking or importing of the marine mammals complies with the principles of the MMPA. If the secretary decides to exempt a certain marine mammal from the moratorium, he must promulgate guidelines and regulations to that effect. The relevant section reads:

> The Secretary ... shall prescribe such regulations with respect to the taking and

importing of animals from each species of marine mammal (including regulations on the taking and importing of individuals within the population stocks) as he deems necessary and appropriate to insure that such taking will not be to the disadvantage of those species and population stocks and will be consistent with the purposes and policies set forth in section 1361 of this title.

Clearly, the secretary has the power to exempt marine mammals from the MMPA's moratorium. Yet the "to insure" and "will be consistent" phrases act as substantial limitations on his discretion.

PENALTIES AND ENFORCEMENT

The MMPA imposes strict penalties for those who violate the moratorium on marine mammals. One found criminally liable may be fined as much as $20,000 and imprisoned for as much as one year, or both. Civil violations are punishable by fines as high as $10,000.

The act is jointly enforced by the Secretary of the Interior and the Justice Department.

3. THE WILD AND FREE-ROAMING HORSES AND BURROS ACT

By 1971 Congress recognized that the number of wild horses and burros was rapidly declining. Hunting and capturing of the animals was the primary reason for the decline. The Congress found that wild horses and burros should be protected because of their historic value and diversity. Consequently, the Wild and Free-Roaming Horses and Burros Act, 16 U.S.C. 1351 (1976), was passed.

The act confers several powers upon the Secretary of the Interior to protect wild horses and burros from being killed or captured. First, the act authorizes the secretary to designate ranges on public lands for the animals. Second, the act requires the secretary to manage the ranges to "maintain a thriving natural economic balance." To maintain this balance the act also requires the secretary to keep inventory of the number of burros and horses on the range. The act punishes any person who attempts to steal, kill, or capture any burro or horse on a range by fines up to $2,000 or up to one year imprisonment, or both.

In 1976 a federal district court in New Mexico held the act to be unconstitutional. The court reasoned that wildlife is the exclusive property of the states, therefore the federal government had no power to regulate wildlife beyond the extent necessary to protect federal lands. The Supreme Court reversed the federal Court's decision in Klepp v. New Mexico, 426 U.S. 529 (1976). The Court decided that since federal power over federal lands was absolute, the federal government had the power to manage the wildlife as it pleased.

4. THE MIGRATORY BIRD TREATY ACT

One of the first major pieces of federal wildlife legislation to be passed in the United States was the Migratory Bird Treaty Act (MBTA), 16 U.S.C. 703 (1976). The MBTA was originally enacted in accordance with a treaty the United States had signed with Canada in 1916. The treaty called for the preservation and protection of cetain migratory birds that both countries found were scarce or becoming extinct. Since 1916, similar treaties have been signed with Mexico and Japan, but the terms of the act have largely remained unchanged.

Unless regulations provide otherwise, the MBTA prohibits any person from chasing, killing, possessing, or selling any bird covered by the treaties. The MBTA confers upon the Secretary of the Interior the power to determine when and how migratory birds may be taken or killed. The secretary's decision must be compatible with the terms of the treaties. In sum, the MBTA gives the federal government the power to regulate the migratory bird population in the United States in accordance with the terms of international treaties.

Chapter 5
HUMANE SLAUGHTER LAWS

Since the turn of the century, the meat industry has grown considerably to satisfy the appetite of an increasing population. Unfortunately, as the industry grew, there was no corresponding growth in the technology of slaughtering animals. Even after World War II, meat packing plants still relied on the archaic methods of slaughtering that they had used decades before. Such methods usually involved hoisting conscious animals into the air by their feet, and cutting their throats. The conclusion reached by many observers was that these practices were highly inhumane and unnecessary. This chapter focuses on the federal legislation that was enacted in order to make the slaughtering process more humane, as well as the state laws that followed.

THE HUMANE SLAUGHTER ACT OF 1958

In 1954, a number of humane organizations began a lobbying effort to urge the federal government to enact humane slaughter legislation. One year later, Senator Hubert Humphrey introduced the first humane slaughter bill ever presented in Congress. In 1958, decades after most European countries had already enacted humane slaughter legislation, Congress finally passed the Humane Slaughter Act (HSA), 7 U.S.C. 1901.

Section 1 of the HSA declares it to be the policy of the United States "that the slaughtering of livestock and the handling of livestock in connection with slaughter shall be carried out only by humane methods."

Section 2 sets forth the methods deemed to be humane. The section reads:

No method of slaughtering or handling in connection with slaughtering shall be deemed to comply with the public policy of the United States unless it is humane. Either of the following two methods of slaughtering and handling are hereby found to be humane:

(a) in the case of cattle, calves, horses, mules, sheep, swine, and other livestock, all animals are rendered insensible to pain by a single blow or gunshot or an electrical, chemical or other means that is rapid and effective, before being shackled, hoisted, thrown, cast, or cut; or

(b) by slaughtering in accordance with the ritual requirements of the Jewish faith or any other religious faith that prescribes a method of slaughter whereby the animal suffers loss of consciousness by anemia of the brain caused by the simultaneous and instantaneous severance of the carotid arteries with a sharp instrument.

The statute, approves of the following methods of rendering an animal insensitive to pain:

1. Carbon Dioxide - Sheep, calves, and swine may be subjected to this method.
2. Gunshot or Mechanical Bolt Stunners - Cattle, calves, swine, goats, and horses may be subjected to this method.
3. Electrical Stunning - Sheep, goats, cattle, calves, and swine may be subjected to this method.

For details, see Regulations to the HSA (Appendix E).

RELIGIOUS EXCEPTIONS

In addition to an express exemption for slaughter in accordance with the Jewish religion, the HSA also exempts any ritual slaughter. Section 1906 states "nothing in this Act shall be construed to prohibit, abridge, or in any way hinder the Religious freedom of any person or group." In other words, the act exempts any slaughtering done in accordance with the requirements of any religion. There are two major reasons for the religious exemption: political pressure and the First Amendment. Prior to passage of the HSA, legislators had commented on the political pressure exerted by various religious groups to provide for a religious exemption. Apparently, the HSA could not have become law without the exemption. The First Amendment, on the other hand, presented a Constitutional problem. The Amendment states that the Government may not pass a law that infringes on the free exercise of religion. It is obvious, that without the religious exemption the HSA would interfere with the slaughter ritual of some religions.

The religious exemption was criticized by humane organizations, which alleged that certain religious slaughter techniques violated the Congressional purpose of the HSA because such techniques were inhumane. For example, kosher slaughter requires that an animal be conscious and uninjured before having its throat slashed. Since agriculture regulations prohibit the cut area of an animal from having contact with the slaughterhouse floor, the animal, while conscious, must be hoisted upside down by shackles before being slaughtered. Obviously the animal undergoes great pain. In the case of Jones v. Butz, 374 F. Supp. 1284 (1974), a federal district court upheld section 1906 as a valid religious exemption from a statutory obligation. Therefore, slaughter done in accordance with the tenets of a religion continues to be exempt.

ADMINISTRATION AND ENFORCEMENT

Since there are no sanctions in the HSA, its administration and enforcement are governed by the provisions of the Federal Meat Inspection ACT (FMIA), 21 USC §601 (1978). Section 610 unequivocally states:

> No person, firm, or corporation shall, with respect to any cattle, sheep, swine, goats, horses, mules, or other equines, or any carcasses, parts of carcasses, meat or meat food products of any such animals –
>
> > – slaughter or handle in connection with slaughter any such animals in any manner not in accordance with the Humane Slaughter Act;
> >
> > – slaughter any such animals or prepare any such articles which are capable for use as Human food at any establishment preparing such articles for commerce, except in compliance with the Humane Slaughter Act.

Furthermore, section 603(b) of the FMIA states that the Secretary of Agriculture is required to inspect slaughtering establishments to determine if they are in compliance with the HSA. The act provides that if the secretary has found that a certain slaughterhouse has not complied with the HSA, inspections are to be halted. Section 610 states that no meat may be

91

sold or transported unless it has been inspected.

Finally, section 620 of the FMIA prohibits the United States from importing any meat that was not slaughtered in accordance with the provisions of the HSA.

STATE LAWS

Although the HSA covers all slaughtering done in the United States, a number of states have enacted their own humane slaughter legislation. such legislation allows the state to have concurrent jurisdiction with the federal government over those who fail to slaughter animals in a humane manner. The great majority of state humane slaughter statutes are very similar to the HSA. In other words, the states often approve the same methods of slaughter as the federal government. Furthermore, states have also incorporated religious exemptions into their statutes. The following states have enacted humane slaughter legislation:

Arizona	Maine
California	Maryland
Colorado	Massachusetts
Connecticut	Michigan
Florida	Minnesota
Georgia	New Hampshire
Illinois	Ohio
Indiana	Oklahoma
Iowa	Oregon
Kansas	Pennsylvania

Rhode Island   Washington
Utah   Wisconsin
Vermont

For a listing of state statute section
numbers see Appendix F.

Chapter 6
REGULATIONS OF TRANSPORTATION
OF ANIMALS

Animal transportation is another area where animals traditionally have suffered. Crowded conditions, inadequate ventilation, lack of food and water, and exposure to heat and cold during transportation have led to the passage of some legislation. This chapter will examine both state and federal attempts to impose humane standards on those who transport animals.

FEDERAL LAW

The Animal Welfare Act, 7 U.S.C. 2131, (1976) requires the Secretary of Agriculture to promulgate regulations setting forth humane standards for animals transported in commerce. Today, the regulations represent the federal government's best attempt to ensure that animals will not be cruelly transported. The federal regulations are divided into different subsections, each referring to a different group of animals. For example, the regulations regarding transportation of dogs and cats are as follows:

No dog or cat may be transported in commerce unless –

1. Cages are sturdy enough to withstand the rigors of transportation;
2. The interior of cages are free from

intrusions that could harm the animals;

3. Cage openings are easily accessible in case of an emergency;
4. Cages are properly ventilated so the animal has sufficient air for normal breathing;
5. Cages must be large enough to ensure that each animal contained therein has sufficient space to turn about freely in a standing position using normal body movements, to stand and sit erect, and to lie in a natural position;
6. Cages are kept clean.
7. Animals are watered at least every 12 hours, and are fed at least once a day;
8. During transportation animals are checked at least every 4 hours; and
9. Animals are not subjected to temperatures under 45° F. nor over 75° F.

The failure to comply with these provisions can subject an animal carrier to up to one year imprisonment and/or a fine up to $1,000. Animal carriers may also have their licenses to transport animals revoked or suspended.

Similar humane standards are also afforded to other species; namely, marine mammals, livestock, rabbits, guinea pigs, hamsters, and primates. However, with so many areas of animal rights law, the problem is not so much as enacting a law as it is enforcing it. Animal transportation laws are no exception. Statistics have shown that the number of inspections of animal carriers has decreased. Consequently, many violators are never identified. Prosecutions are even more rare. Out of seventy-one administrative proceedings filed between 1966 and 1976, only six resulted in license revocations. Furthermore, license revocations are not permanent. Once an animal carrier has had his license revoked he may apply for another after one year.

STATE LAWS

In addition to federal legislation, most states have enacted laws prohibiting the inhumane transport of animals. Many states have expressly held inhumane transport of animals to be a violation of that State's Anti-cruelty law. Other states have only enacted statutes regulating the transport of livestock. If a state does not prohibit cruel transport, a person might still be found guilty of cruelty under that state's anti-cruelty statute. Below is a listing of state laws regulating the transportation of animals. For a listing of state statute section numbers see Appendix G.

ALABAMA

The Alabama Anti-Cruelty Statute does not expressly prohibit cruel transportation of animals. However, the state has enacted a statute concerning the humane transportation of livestock. The statute begins by stating:

> "It shall be unlawful in this State to handle or transport livestock in any manner not consistent with humane methods of treatment to such extent as is reasonably possible ..."

The statute requires that livestock be transported by way of the most direct route so as to prevent delay. Vehicles used to transport livestock must be constructed so that the roof of the vehicle will not touch the highest point of the back of any animal. Animals transported in vehicles run by diesel fuel must be protected from breathing the exhaust fumes.

Any person who violates the above prohibitions will be guilty of a misdemeanor. The penalty is up to six months imprisonment and/or a $100 fine.

ARKANSAS

Arkansas expressly prohibits any person from transporting an animal in a cruel manner. Any person who violates this law is guilty of a misdemeanor punishable by a maximum of one year imprisonment and/or a $1,000 fine.

CALIFORNIA

California has enacted a statute prohibiting anyone from transporting any domestic animal in a cruel manner. Violation of the statute is a misdemeanor punishable by a maximum of six months imprisonment and/or up to a $500 fine. California has also enacted laws regarding the transportation of livestock. California prohibits any person from keeping any animal in a truck for more than 28 hours. An animal may be kept for 36 hours if certain conditions exist. On trains, animals must not be transported for more than 36 hours. Animals must be given at least five hours of rest after 28 hours on trucks or 36 hours on trains.

COLORADO

Any person who transports an animal in a cruel manner in Colorado is guilty of cruelty to animals. The penalty is as high as two years in jail and/or a $500 fine.

CONNECTICUT

Like Colorado, Connecticut makes it illegal for anyone to carry an animal in a cruel manner. The penalty is up to one year imprisonment and/or a $250 fine.

Connecticut law also prohibits animals transported by train to remain confined for more than 28 hours, except when transported in cars in which they have proper food, water, and space for rest. Otherwise animals must be unloaded and rested for at least five hours. Any person found to violate this section may be fined up to $500 dollars.

DISTRICT OF COLUMBIA

The District of Columbia makes no provision for animal transportation in its cruelty statute. However, in regard to livestock, it prohibits railroad companies from transporting animals for more than 24 hours, without at least five hours of rest, food, and water. If, however, animals are given proper food, water, and space for rest on the train, then the 24-hour limit will not apply. Failure to comply with the law could result in a fine as high as $500 dollars.

FLORIDA

In Florida, any person who transports an animal in an unnecessarily cruel manner is guilty of cruelty to animals. It is punishable by a maximum of one year imprisonment and/or a $1,000 fine. Florida also prohibits any transportation company from transporting livestock for more than 28 hours without feeding, watering, or resting. The penalty is up to 60 days imprisonment and/or a $500 fine.

HAWAII

In Hawaii, any person who knowingly or recklessly transports any creature in a cruel manner is guilty of cruelty to animals. It is punishable by up to a $1,000 fine or one year imprisonment.

IDAHO

In Idaho, the law prohibits anyone from transporting any animal in a cruel manner. The penalty is up to six months imprisonment and/or a $300 fine.

ILLINOIS

In Illinois, any transporter of animals is prohibited from transporting an animal for more than 28 hours without, food, water, rest, and exercise. The penalty for non-compliance is up to a $500 fine.

LOUISIANA

In Louisiana, a person is guilty of cruelty to animals if he transports an animal in a cruel or inhumane manner. The penalty is up to six months imprisonment or a $1,000 fine. Additionally, transporters of livestock are required to provide an adequate water supply for animals to drink as they are loaded and unloaded on trains.

MAINE

Maine has enacted a thorough animal transportation law. In addition to prohibiting transportation in excess of 28 hours without food, water, and rest, the law states:

Railroad companies within the State

shall give cars containing cattle, sheep, swine or other animals a continuous passage in preference to other freight. Cars loaded with such animals at any station shall have precedence over all other freight. A greater number of animals shall not be loaded into any car than can stand comfortably in the same apartment. Young animals shall not be loaded in the same apartment with those larger and mature, except in case of dams with their own and other sucklings, which shall in all cases be transported in the same apartment and separate from other animals. Calves shall have free access to their dams and shall not be muzzled, except that calves, for a period not to exceed 24 hours, may be transported in a separate compartment. During December, January, February and March, cars used for the transportation of animals shall be sufficiently boarded on the sides and ends to afford proper protection to such animals in case of storms or severe cold weather. A railroad company or other transportation line violating any provision of this section forfeits not less that $50 nor more than $500 for every such offense.

MASSACHUSETTS

In Massachusetts, a person is guilty of cruelty to animals if he transports an animal in an unnecessarily cruel manner, or in a manner which might endanger the animal. The penalty is a maximum of one year imprisonment and/or a $500 fine. Massachusetts also requires that no animal be confined in any railroad car for more than 28 hours without at least five hours of rest, food, and water. The penalty for noncompliance is a fine as high as $500.

MICHIGAN

The Michigan statute is more specific than most. The statute makes it a misdemeanor for any person to:

> Carry or cause to be caried any live animal in or upon any vehicle or otherwise without providing suitable racks, cars, crates or cages, in which such animal may stand or lie down during transportation, and while awaiting slaughter....

The penalty is up to 90 days imprisonment and/or a $100 fine.

Michigan law also prohibits any railroad company from confining an animal for more than 36 hours without at least five hours of rest, food and water. The penalty for failure to comply is as high as $500.

MINNESOTA

Minnesota has enacted a very specific statute. No person may:

1.   Transport an animal in any vehicle

without providing suitable racks, crates, cars or cages in which the animal can stand and lie down; or

2. Transport or detain livestock in cars for more than 28 hours without unloading the livestock for at least five hours for food, water and rest; or

3. Permit livestock to be crowded together without sufficient space to stand, or so as to overlie, crush, wound or kill each other.

The penalty for violating any of the above provisions is up to 90 days imprisonment and/or a $500 fine.

MISSOURI

Missouri makes it a misdemeanor for any person to transport any animal in a cruel or inhumane manner. The penalty for doing so is up to one year imprisonment and/or up to a $1,000 fine.

MONTANA

In Montana, a person is guilty of cruelty to animals if he knowingly or negligently subjects an animal to mistreatment by carrying it in a cruel manner. The penalty is up to six months imprisonment or up to a $1,000 fine.

NEVADA

The Nevada Cruelty Statute prohibits any person from transporting an animal in a cruel manner, or so as to produce torture. The penalty is up to six months imprisonment and/or a $500 fine. The law also requires that animals not be transported for more than 28 hours without being unloaded to rest, eat, and drink.

NEW HAMPSHIRE

In New Hampshire, a person is guilty of a misdemeanor if he transports any animal "in a manner injurious to the health, safety or physical well-being of such animal." The penalty is up to one year imprisonment and/or a $1,000 fine.

NEW JERSEY

In New Jersey, any person who transports an animal in a cruel or inhumane manner is guilty of a misdemeanor punishable by up to six months imprisonment and/or a $250 fine.

NEW MEXICO

New Mexico requires that livestock transported by truck and confined for 36 hours without rest, feed, or water be given at least four hours of rest, and feed and water.

NEW YORK

New York law prohibits any person from transporting any animal in a cruel manner, or so as to produce torture. The penalty is up to one year imprisonment and/or a $500 fine. Additionally, livestock animals are not to be transported for more than 28 hours without unloading for rest, water, and feeding. The resting period must be for a minimum of five hours.

NORTH CAROLINA

In North Carolina, it is a misdemeanor for any person to transport an animal in a cruel manner. The penalty is up to six months imprisonment and/or a $100 fine.

NORTH DAKOTA

The North Dakota Transportation Statute reads:
> No person shall carry, or cause to be carried, any live animals upon any vehicle or otherwise, without providing suitable racks, cars, crates, or cages, or other proper carrying container, nor shall he carry an animal, or cause an animal to be carried, in any other cruel manner.

The penalty is a maximum of one year imprisonment and/or a $1,000 fine.

OHIO

Like many states, Ohio prohibits any person from transporting an animal in a cruel manner. Ohio also requires that animals be given exercise, change of air, food, and water after 28 hours of travel. The penalty for failure to comply is up to 90 days imprisonment and/or a $750 fine.

OKLAHOMA

Oklahoma, like many other states, prohibits any person from transporting an animal in a cruel manner, or so as to produce torture. The penalty is up to one year imprisonment and/or a $500 fine.

OREGON

Oregon law prohibits any person from transporting an animal in a cruel or inhumane manner. The penalty is up to six months imprisonment and/or a $500 fine.

PENNSYLVANIA

The Pennsylvania Transportation Statute reads:

> A person commits a summary offense if he carries, or causes, or allows to be caried in or upon any cart, or other vehicle whatsoever, any animal in a cruel or inhumane manner.

The penalty is a maximum of 90 days imprisonment and/or $300 fine.

RHODE ISLAND

In Rhode Island, any person who transports an animal in a cruel or inhumane manner is guilty of cruelty to animals. The penalty is a maximum of 11 months imprisonment and/or a $250 fine. Rhode Island law also requires railroads to give animals at least five hours of rest for every 28 hours traveled. Failure to do so can result in a fine up to $500 dollars for every offense.

SOUTH CAROLINA

South Carolina prohibits any person from transporting an animal in a cruel manner. The penalty is up to 30 days imprisonment and/or a $100 fine. South Carolina also requires railroads to give animals at least five hours rest for every 36 hours traveled. Failure to do so can result in a fine as high as $500.

TENNESSEE

The Tennessee law reads:
- If any person shall carry or cause to be carried in or upon any vehicle or other conveyance any creature in a cruel or inhumane manner, he shall be guilty of a misdemeanor.

The penalty is up to one year imprisonment

and/or a $1,000 fine.

TEXAS

In Texas, a person will be guilty of cruelty to animals if he intentionally or knowingly transports an animal in a cruel manner. The penalty for cruelty is up to one year imprisonment and/or a $2,000 fine.

UTAH

Utah has enacted the same wording as that of Texas. The penalty however, is smaller: up to six months imprisonment and/or a $299 fine.

VERMONT

Like many other states, Vermont prohibits any person from transporting an animal in an unnecessarily cruel manner. The penalty is up to one year imprisonment and/or up to a $200 fine. Vermont also requires that animals transported by railroad be given at least five hours rest after 28 hours of travel. Failure to comply can result in a fine as high as $200. Additionally, Vermont prohibits animals from being confined in any truck for more than 18 hours without at least a four-hour rest period. This offense is punishable by up to $100.

VIRGINIA

Any person who transports an animal in a cruel manner in Virginia is guilty of cruelty to

animals.   The penalty is up to one year
imprisonment and/or a $1,000 fine. The Virginia
Animal Welfare Act also requires that no animal
transporter may transport animals for more than
28 hours without rest, food, water, and exercise.

WASHINGTON

The Washington statute reads:

Any person who willfully transports or
confines or causes to be transported or
confined any domestic animal or animals in
a manner, posture or confinement that will
jeopardize the safety of the animal or the
public shall be guilty of a misdemeanor.

The penalty is up to 60 days imprisonment
and/or a $150 fine. Washington also imposes a
$100 fine on railroads that fail to rest animals
after 48 consecutive hours of travel.

WEST VIRGINIA

West Virginia law prohibits any person
from transporting an animal in a cruel or
inhumane manner. The penalty is a maximum of
six months imprisonment and/or a $100 fine.

WISCONSIN

Like many other states, Wisconsin prohibits
any person from transporting an animal in a
cruel manner. The penalty is a maximum of one
year imprisonment and/or a $500 fine.

WYOMING

Like Wisconsin, Wyoming prohibits any person from transporting an animal in a cruel or inhumane manner. The penalty is up to one year imprisonment and/or a $100 fine.

Chapter 7
SUGGESTIONS FOR IMPROVEMENT

Although increased enforcement of existing animal welfare laws is necessary, the statutes themselves could be amended in several respects to strengthen protection for animals. For example, anti-cruelty statutes may be too broad. Virtually every statute prohibits cruelty that is unjustified or unnecessary. Is a person justified in beating his dog because it barked too early in the morning? Is it necessary that a cat be beaten for urinating on a rug? Perhaps it is possible that these subjective terms be deleted from the anti-cruelty statutes and replaced with more objective guidelines.

Additionally state cruelty laws should be amended or interpreted to require lower levels of intent for conviction. Too many states require cruelty be committed "intentionally" or with "malice." Both levels of intent are very difficult to prove. By requiring "recklessness" or "criminal negligence" a statute can convict many more types of cruelty. States should adopt these lower levels of intent to make their cruelty statutes more effective.

Critics of laboratory animal law believe that researchers should not be given complete discretion in animal experimentation. If a particular experiment was adequately performed on ten dogs in 1983, is it necessary that the same experiment take place on ten more dogs in 1984? Perhaps a national data bank could be created to inform researchers of those experiments that have already been completed. Animal rights groups are fighting to amend the Animal Welfare Act. However, researchers and medical institutions represent a powerful force in this country that must be dealt with.

Until more states enact laws prohibiting pound seizure, as New York has done, many impounded animals will continue to wind up in laboratories. The lack of uniformity among states in pound seizure legislation permits research institutions in states that have prohibited pound seizures to obtain animals from neighboring states where pound seizure is still legal.

Laws regulating trapping could also be tightened, especially regarding the types of traps to be employed. For example, there are traps that can either capture an animal without harming it, or kill it instantly. Although such traps are more expensive, over fifty countries have banned the traditional leghold trap and adopted these more humane traps. Isn't it time the United States did so as well?

Animal fighting laws could be improved by increasing penalties for those responsible for instituting the fight. Animal fighting must be stopped at its source. Today, most states still punish spectators to the same extent as those who conduct the fight. Persons who witness and bet on animal fights should continue to be punished. But if these fights are to be stopped completely, the punishment for promoters must be increased.

A major problem with humane slaughter legislation is the religious exemption. While kosher slaughter techniques may have been considered humane two thousand years ago, they are not considered humane today. Perhaps such exemptions should be eliminated.

Finally, humane transportation statutes, like anti-cruelty statutes, must be made more specific. Almost every State expressly prohibits transporting animals in a cruel or inhumane manner. What seems cruel to one person may seem perfectly fine to another. Is it cruel to transport a large dog in a cage in which it can't even stand? Is it inhumane to continue transporting a dog after it has been repeatedly sick from motion sickness? As the transportation statutes stand today, they are, at best, quite vague.

To achieve these changes, animal rights supporters must make their presence known to the legislature. The key to being heard is organization and properly applied political pressure. When law makers believe there is enough of an interest in animal welfare, they will act. Until that time comes, animals will remain a largely unprotected part of our society.

APPENDIXES
Appendix A
State Anti-Cruelty Laws

STATE	SECTION
ALABAMA	13A-11-14
ALASKA	11-61.140
ARIZONA	13-2910
ARKANSAS	41-2918
CALIFORNIA	Penal 597
COLORADO	18-9-202,35-42-112
CONNECTICUT	53-247
DELAWARE	11-1325
DISTRICT OF COL.	22-801
FLORIDA	828.12
GEORGIA	16-12-4
HAWAII	37-711-1110
IDAHO	18-2102
ILLINOIS	8-704
INDIANA	35-46-3-2
IOWA	717.1,717.2
KANSAS	21-4310
KENTUCKY	525.130
LOUISIANA	14:102,1
MAINE	17A-510
MARYLAND	27-59
MASSACHUSETTS	272-77
MICHIGAN	752.21
MINNESOTA	343.20
MISSISSIPPI	97-41-1
MISSOURI	578.055
MONTANA	45-8-211
NEBRASKA	28-1002
NEVADA	574.100
NEW HAMPSHIRE	644:8

NEW JERSEY	4:22-17
NEW MEXICO	30-18-1,30-18-2
NEW YORK	Agri: & Mkt. 353
NORTH CAROLINA	14-360
NORTH DAKOTA	36-21.1-02
OHIO	959.13
OKLAHOMA	21-1685
OREGON	167.850
PENNSYLVANIA	18-5511
RHODE ISLAND	4-1-2
SOUTH CAROLINA	47-1-40
SOUTH DAKOTA	40-1-2
TENNESSEE	39-3-104
TEXAS	Penal 42.11
UTAH	76-9-301
VERMONT	13-403
VIRGINIA	18.2-392
WASHINGTON	16.52.070
WEST VIRGINIA	61-8-19
WISCONSIN	948.02
WYOMING	11-29-102

§2131. Congressional statement of policy

The Congress finds that animals and activities which are regulated under this Act [7 USC §§2131 et seq.] are either in interstate or foreign commerce or substantially affect such commerce or the free flow thereof, and that regulation of animals and activities as provided in this Act [7 USCS §§2131 et seq.] is necessary to prevent and eliminate burdens upon such commerce and to effectively regulate such commerce, in order —

> (1) to insure that animals intended for use in research facilities or for exhibition purposes or for use as pets are provided humane care and treatment;
>
> (2) to assure the humane treatment of animals during transportation in commerce; and
>
> (3) to protect the owners of animals from the theft of their animals by preventing the sale or use of animals which have been stolen.

The Congress further finds that it is esssential to regulate, as provided in this Act [7 USCS §§2131 et seq.], the transportation, purchase, sale, housing, care, handling, and treatment of animals by carriers or by persons or organizations engaged in using them for research or experimental purposes or for exhibiting purposes or holding them for sale as pets or for any such purpose or use.

§2133. Licensing of dealers and exhibitors

The Secretary shall issue licenses to dealers and exhibitors upon application therefor in such form and manner as he may prescribe and upon payment of such fee established pursuant to section 23 of this Act [7 USC §2153]: Provided, that no such license shall be issued until the dealer or exhibitor shall have demonstrated that his facitities comply with the standards promulgated by the Secretary pursuant to section 13 of this Act [7 USC §2143]: Provided, however, that any retail pet store or other person who derives less than a substantial portion of his income (as determined by the Secretary) from the breeding and raising of dogs or cats on his own premises and sells any such dog or cat to a dealer or research facility shall not be required to obtain a license as a dealer or exhibitor under this Act [7 USC §§2131 et seq.]. The Secretary is further authorized to License, as dealers or exhibitors, persons who do not qualify as dealers or exhibitors within the meaning of this Act [7 USC §§2131 et seq.] upon such persons' complying with the requirements specified above and agreeing, in writing, to comply with all the requirements of this Act [7 USC §§2131 et seq.] and the regulations promulgated by the Secretary hereunder.

§2134. Valid license for dealers and exhibitors required

No dealer or exhibitor shall sell or offer to see or transport or offer for transportation, in commerce, to any research facility or for exhibition or for use as a pet any animal, or buy, sell, offer to buy or sell, transport or offer for transportation, in commerce, to or from another dealer or exhibitor under this Act [7 USC §§2131 et seq.] any animal, unless and until such dealer or exhibitor shall have obtained a license from the Secretary and such license shall not have been suspended or revoked.

§2135. Time period for disposal of dogs or cats by dealers or exhibitors

No dealer or exhibitor shall sell or otherwise dispose of any dog or cat within a period of five business days after the acquisition of such animal or within such other period as may be specified by the Secretary: Provided, that operators of auction sales subject to section 12 of this Act [7 USC §2142] shall not be required to comply with the provisions of this section.

§2136. Registration of research facilities, handlers, carriers and unlicensed exhibitors

Every research facility, every intermediate handler, every carrier, and every exhibitor not licensed under section 3 of this Act [7 USC §2133] shall register with the Secretary in accordance with such rules and regulations as he may prescribe.

§2137. Purchase of dogs or cats by research facilities prohibited except from authorized operators of auction sales and licensed dealers or exhibitors

It shall be unlawful for any research facility to purchase any dog or cat from any person except an operator of an auction sale subject to section 12 of this Act [7 USC §2142] or a person holding a valid license as a dealer or exhibitor issued by the Secretary pursuant to this Act [7 USC §§ 2131 et seq.] unless such person is exempted from obtaining such license under section 3 of this Act [7 USC §2133].

§2140. Record keeping by dealers, exhibitors, research facilites, intermediate handlers, and carriers

Dealers and exhibitors shall make and retain for such reasonable period of time as the Secretary may prescribe, such records with respect to the purchase, sale, transportation, identification, and previous ownership of animals as the Secretary may prescribe. Research facilities shall make and retain such records only with respect to the purchase, sale, transportation, identification and previous ownership of live dogs and cats. At the request of the Secretary, any regulatory agency of the Federal Government which requires records to be maintained by intermediate handlers and carriers with respect to the transportation, receiving, handling, and delivery of animals on forms prescribed by the agency, shall require there to be included in such forms, and intermediate handlers and carriers shall include in such forms, such information as the Secretary may require for the effective administration of this Act [7 USC §§2131 et seq.]. Such information shall be retained for such reasonable period of time as the Secretary may prescribe. If regulatory agencies of the Federal Government do not prescribe requirements for any such forms, intermediate handlers and carriers shall make and retain for such reasonable period as the Secretary may prescribe such records with respect to the transportation, receiving, handling, and delivery of animals as the Secretary may prescribe such records with respect to the transportation, receiving, handling, and delivery of animals as the Secretary may prescribe. Such records shall be made available at all reasonable times for inspection and copying by the Secretary.

§2141. Marking and identification of animals

All animals delivered for transportation, transported, purchased, or sold, in commerce, by a dealer or exhibitor shall be marked or identified at such time and in such manner as the Secretary may prescribe: provided, that only live dogs and cats need be so marked or identified by a research facility.

§2142. Humane standards and record keeping requirements at auction sales.

The Secretary is authorized to promulgate humane standards and record keeping requirements governing the purchase, handling, or sale of animals, in commerce, by dealers, research facilities, and exhibitors at auction sales and by the operators of such auction sales. The Secretary is also authorized to require the licensing of operators of auction sales where any dogs or cats are sold, in commerce, under such conditions as he may prescribe, and upon payment of such fee as prescribed by the Secretary under section 23 of this Act [7 USCS §2153].

§2143. Humane standards for animals transported in commerce.

(a) Authority of Secretary to promulgate standards. The Secretary shall promulgate standards to govern the humane handling, care, treatment, and transportation of animals by dealers, research facilities, and exhibitors. Such standards shall include minimum requirements with respect to handling, housing, feeding, watering, sanitation, ventilation, shelter from extremes of weather and temperatures, adequate veterinary care, including the appropriate use of anesthetic, analgesic or tranquilizing drugs, when such use would be proper in the opinion of the attending veterinarian of such research facilities, and separation by species when the Secretary finds such separation necessary for the humane handling, care, or treatment of animals. The Secretary shall also promulgate standards to govern the transportation in commerce, and the handling, care, and treatment in connection therewith, by intermediate handlers, air carriers, or other carriers, of animals consigned by any dealer, research facility, exhibitor, operator of an auction sale, or other person, or any department, agency or instrumentality of the United States or of any State or local government, for transportation in commerce. The Secretary shall have authority to promulgate such rules and regulations as he determines necessary to assure humane treatment of animals in the course of their transportation in commerce including requirements such as those with respect to containers, feed, water, rest, ventilation, temperature, and handling. In promulgating and enforcing standards established pursuant to this section, the Secretary is authorized and directed to consult experts, including outside consultants where indicated. Nothing in this Act [7 USC §§ 2131 et seq.] shall be construed as authorizing the Secretary to promulgate rules, regulations, or orders with regard to design, outlines, guidelines, or performance of actual research or experimentation by a research facility as determined by such research facility: Provided, that the Secretary shall require, at least annually, every research facility to show that professionally acceptable standards governing the care, treatment, and use of animals, including appropriate use of anesthetic, analgesic, and tranquilizing drugs, during experimentation are being followed by the research facility during actual research or experimentation.

Appendix C
Selected Animal Trapping

ALABAMA	9-11-266, 9-11-254
ALASKA	16.05.195
ARIZONA	17-361
ARKANSAS	47-316
CALIFORNIA	Fish and Game 4000-4011
COLORADO	33-22-101 to 108
CONNECTICUT	26-72
DELAWARE	7-704, 706
FLORIDA	372.57
GEORGIA	27-3-62
IDAHO	36-1103
ILLINOIS	61-2.30
INDIANA	14-2-4-2
IOWA	109.87, 109.92
KANSAS	32-158
KENTUCKY	150.399-410
LOUISIANA	56.261
MAINE	12§7431-32
MARYLAND	Nat. Res. 10-408:1
MASSACHUSETTS	131 80
MICHIGAN	313.1
MINNESOTA	100.29
MISSISSIPPI	49-7-13
MONTANA	87-3-127,501,107
NEBRASKA	37-610
NEVADA	503.440
NEW HAMPSHIRE	210:1
NEW JERSEY	23:4-20
NEW MEXICO	17-5-1 to 17-5-9
NEW YORK	ECL-11-1101
NORTH CAROLINA	113.291.6

NORTH DAKOTA	20.1-07
OHIO	1533
OKLAHOMA	29 §5-502
OREGON	497.075, 497.142
PENNSYLVANIA	34-1311.601
RHODE ISLAND	20-16-8.
SOUTH CAROLINA	15-11-1510
SOUTH DAKOTA	41-8-19 to 22
TENNESSEE	51-439
TEXAS	72.001
UTAH	23-18-2
VERMONT	10 §44
VIRGINIA	29-143
WASHINGTON	77.20
WEST VIRGINIA	20-2-17
WISCONSIN	29.13
WYOMING	23-2-303

Appendix D
Animal Fighting Laws

STATE	SECTION
ALABAMA	13A-12-4
ALASKA	11.61.145
ARIZONA	13-2910.01
ARKANSAS	41-2918
CALIFORNIA	Penal 597.5,597b
COLORADO	35-42-113,18-9-204
CONNECTICUT	53-247
DELAWARE	28-904
DISTRICT OF COL.	22-809
FLORIDA	828.121
GEORGIA	16-12-4
HAWAII	37-711-1109
IDAHO	18-2104
ILLINOIS	8:704.01
INDIANA	35-46-3-2
IOWA	717.3,725.11
KENTUCKY	525.130
MAINE	17-A-510
MASSACHUSETTS	272-88
MICHIGAN	750.49
MINNESOTA	343.31
MISSISSIPPI	97-41-11
MISSOURI	578-050
MONTANA	45-8-211
NEVADA	574.060
NEW HAMPSHIRE	644:8-a
NEW JERSEY	4:22-24
NEW YORK	Ag. 2 MKT 351
NORTH CAROLINA	14-362

NORTH DAKOTA	36-21.1-07
OHIO	959:15
OKLAHOMA	21:1682,1683
OREGON	167.865
PENNSYLVANIA	18:5511
RHODE ISLAND	4-1-9
SOUTH CAROLINA	16-17-650
SOUTH DAKOTA	40-1-9
TENNESSEE	39-3-105
TEXAS	Penal 42.11
UTAH	76-9-301
VERMONT	13:410
VIRGINIA	18.2-394
WASHINGTON	16.52.120
WEST VIRGINIA	61-8-19
WISCONSIN	948.08
WYOMING	11-29-112

Appendix E
Selected Sections of Federal Regulations
to the Humane Slaughter Act

TITLE 9 §313

§313.5 Chemical; carbon dioxide.

The slaughtering of sheep, calves and swine with the use of carbon dioxide gas and the handling in connection therewith, in compliance with the provisions contained in this section, are hereby designated and approved as humane methods of slaughtering and handling of such animals under the Act.

(a) Administration of gas, required effect; handling.
(1) The carbon dioxide gas shall be administered in a chamber in accordance with this section so as to produce surgical anesthesia in the animals before they are shackled, hoisted, thrown, cast, or cut. The animals shall be exposed to the carbon dioxide gas in a way that will accomplish the anesthesia quickly and calmly, with a minimum of excitement and discomfort to the animals.

§313.15 Mechanical; captive bolt.

The slaughtering of sheep, swine, goats,

calves, cattle, horses, mules, and other equines by using captive bolt stunners and the handling in connection therewith, in compliance with the provisions contained in this section, are hereby designated and approved as humane methods of slaughtering and handling of such animals under the Act.

(a) Application of stunners, required effect; handling.
(1) The captive bolt stunners shall be applied to the livestock in accordance with this section so as to produce immediate unconsciousness in the animals before they are shackled, hoisted, thrown, cast, or cut. The animals shall be stunned in such a manner that they will be rendered unconscious with a minimum of excitement and discomfort.

§313.16 Mechanical; gunshot.

The slaughtering of cattle, calves, sheep, swine, goats, horses, mules, and other equines by shooting with firearms and the handling in connection therewith, in compliance with the provisions contained in this section, are hereby designated and approved as humane methods of slaughtering and handling of such animals under the Act.

(a) Utilization of firearms, required effect; handling.
(1) The firearms shall be employed in the delivery of a bullet or projectile into the

animal in accordance with this section so as to produce immediate unconsciousness in the animal by a single shot before it is shackled, hoisted, thrown, cast, or cut. The animals shall be shot in such a manner that they will be rendered unconscious with a minimum of excitement and discomfort.

Appendix F
State Humane Slaughter Laws

STATE	SECTION NO.
ARIZONA	24-661
CALIFORNIA	Agricultural Code 19501
COLORADO	35-58-107
CONNECTICUT	22-272A
FLORIDA	828.24
GEORGIA	26-2-110.1
ILLINOIS	8-229.51
INDIANA	16-6-5-8
IOWA	189A.18
KANSAS	47-1403
MAINE	22-2554
MARYLAND	27-333B
MASSACHUSETTS	94-139D
MICHIGAN	287.552,287.553
MINNESOTA	31.591
NEW HAMPSHIRE	575-A:2
OHIO	945.01
OKLAHOMA	2-1053
OREGON	603.065
PENNSYLVANIA	3-451.52
RHODE ISLAND	4-17-3,4-17-4
UTAH	4-27-5(F)
VERMONT	6§3131
WASHINGTON	16.50.120
WISCONSIN	95.80

Appendix G
State Animal Transportation Laws

STATE	SECTION
ALABAMA	13A-11-14/2-15-110
ARKANSAS	41-2955
CALIFORNIA	Penal 597a
	Agric. 16905-08
COLORADO	18-9-202,35-42-112
CONNECTICUT	53-247,53-252
DISTRICT OF COL.	22-803
FLORIDA	828.12, 828.14
HAWAII	37-711-1110
IDAHO	18-2103
ILLINOIS	8-707
LOUISIANA	14:102.1, 45:481
MAINE	17A-510, 17-1172
MASSACHUSETTS	272-77, 272-81
MICHIGAN	750.51
MINNESOTA	343.20, 343.24
MISSOURI	578.060
MONTANA	45-8-211
NEVADA	574.100, 705.090
NEW HAMPSHIRE	644:8
NEW JERSEY	4:22-17
NEW MEXICO	77-9-63
NEW YORK	Agri: & Mkt. 359
NORTH CAROLINA	14-363
NORTH DAKOTA	36-21.1-02
OHIO	959.13
OKLAHOMA	21-1688
OREGON	167.860
PENNSYLVANIA	18-5511(e)

RHODE ISLAND	4-1-3,4-1-17
SOUTH CAROLINA	47-1-50
TENNESSEE	39-3-108
TEXAS	Penal 42.11 39-3-108
UTAH	76-9-301
VERMONT	13-403,13-461,13-462
VIRGINIA	18.2-392,-3.1-796.43
WASHINGTON	16.52.080/81.56.130
WEST VIRGINIA	61-8-19
WISCONSIN	948.02 948.05
WYOMING	11-29-102

Appendix H
Edward Taub v. State of Maryland

On August 10, 1983, a major case was decided concerning the issue of whether state anti-cruelty laws could apply to laboratory researchers who mistreat animals. The case involved the appeal of Dr. Edward Taub, the chief scientific investigator in charge of animal research at the Institute for Behavioral Research in Silver Springs, Maryland.

Dr. Taub was convicted of violating the Maryland anti-cruelty statute. In 1981, Taub conducted research to gain information to help retrain human beings afflicted with a stroke. In an effort to learn how to retrain limbs damaged by a stroke, Taub simulated the effects of a stroke by creating an animal model of the conditions in humans. Taub did so by surgically abolishing all sensation in the limbs of several monkeys. Thereafter Taub was accused of grossly neglecting the monkeys.

A former employee of the laboratory informed police of the conditions at Dr. Taub's laboratory. County police investigated the laboratory, seized several monkeys, and charged Dr. Taub with violating the state's anti-cruelty statute. In the lower court, Taub was found guilty of cruelty to animals. On his first appeal Taub's conviction was affirmed. Specifically it was found Taub failed to give proper veterinary care to one monkey. However, on appeal, the state's highest court reversed Taub's conviction. An edited version of the decision follows below:

Edward Taub v. State of Maryland
No. 123, September Term, 1982
Court of Appeals of Maryland
August 10, 1983

Opinion by Couch, J.

The Issue in this case is whether the animal cruelty statute, Maryland Code (1957, 1976 Repl. Vol.), Article 27 § 59, is applicable to a research institute conducting medical and scientific research pursuant to a federal program. For reasons to be discussed herein we hold that it is not....

While Dr. Taub has raised several issues concerning the constitutionality of section 59, preemption of this section by the Federal Act, and certain alleged errors in the trial court's evidentiary rulings, we believe the matter may be disposed of by our conclusion that section 59 simply is inapplicable to Dr. Taub and the laboratory and thus the charges against him should be dismissed.

By Chapter 198 of the Laws of Maryland, 1890, the legislature, for the first time, made it a misdemeanor for
> any person who wilfully sets on foot, instigates, engages in, or in any way furthers any act of cruelty to any animal, or any act tending to produce such cruelty,

136

or by any act, conduct, neglect, or omission wilfully causes, permits or suffers any animal to undergo any species of torture or cruelty....

Torture and cruelty were thereafter defined "to include everything whereby unjustifiable physical pain, suffering, or death [w]as caused or permitted...." (Emphasis added.)

In 1904 this chapter became sections 57 and 58 of Article 27 without change. The next legislative action of significance, pertinent to the issue before us, occurred in 1955, Chapter 19, when a specific penalty for violation of the section was provided by Chapter 718 of the Laws of 1963, the penalty provision was changed to provide for up to ninety days imprisonment. The legislature increased the fine provision to $1,000.00 in 1966, by Chapter 333. In 1972, by Chapter 719, the legislature repealed the pertinent sections and enacted a new section 59 to read as follows:

Any person who (1) overdrives, overloads, deprives of necessary sustenance, tortures, torments, cruelly beats, mutilates or cruelly kills; or (2) causes, procures or authorizes these acts; or (3) having the charge or custody of an animal, either as owner or otherwise, inflicts unnecessary suffering or pain upon the animal, or unnecessarily fails to provide the animal with proper food, drink, air space, shelter or protection from the weather, is guilty....

Section 62 was amended to define "torment," otherwise it remained essentially unchanged. In

1975, by Chapter 716, section 59 was repealed and reenacted with the language as it was at the time of the inception of this case, as set forth below:

Any person who (1) overdrives, overloads, deprives of necessary sustenance, tortures, torments, cruelly beats, mutilates or cruelly kills; or (2) causes, procures or authorizes these acts; or (3) having the charge or custody of an animal, either as owner or otherwise, inflicts unnecessary suffering or pain upon the animal, or unnecessarily fails to provide the animal with nutritious food in sufficient quantity, necessary veterinary care, proper drink, air, space, shelter, or protection from the weather, is guilty of a misdemeanor and shall be punishable by a fine not exceeding $1,000 or by imprisonment not to exceed 90 days or both. Customary and normal veterinary and agricultural husbandry practices including but not limited to dehorning, castration, docking tails, and limit feeding, are not covered by the provisions of this section.

In the case of activities in which physical pain may unavoidably be caused to animals, such as food processing, pest elimination, animal training, and hunting, cruelty shall mean a failure to employ the most humane method reasonably available. It is the intention of the General Assembly that all animals shall be protected from intentional cruelty, but that no person shall be liable for criminal prosecution for normal human activities to which the infliction of pain to an animal is purely incidental and unavoidable.

It can readily be seen that the legislature has consistently been concerned with the punishment of acts causing "unnecessary" or "unjustifiable" pain or suffering. Furthermore, clearly the legislature recognized that there are certain normal human activities to which the infliction of pain to an animal is purely incidental and unavoidable and, in such instances, section 59 does not apply.

In addition, we are confident that the legislature was aware of the Federal Animal Welfare Act which was, in part, to insure that animals intended for use in research facilities would be provided humane care and treatment. Under the terms of that Act, a research facility is required to register with the Secretary of Agriculture (7 U.S.C. § 2136, (1973, 1976 Supp.)), to comply with standards promulgated by the Secretary to govern the humane handling, care, and treatment of animals (§ 2143 (1976 Supp.)), is subject to inspection of their penalties, as well as a cease and desist order for any violation of the Act (§2149(b) and (c) (1976 Supp.)). Thus the Act provides a comprehensive plan for the protection of animals used in research facilities, while at the same time recognizing and preserving the validity of use of animals in research (§ 2146 (1973 and 1976 Supp.)).

139

Moreover, the involved laboratory was subject to detailed regulations of the Secretary of Agriculture (9 C.F.R. §§ 3.75-391 (1978)) which set forth specifications for humane handling, care, treatment, transportation of nonhuman primateds, and for veterinary care. With respect to the latter, again provision is made for a recognition and preservation of the validity of research purposes.

Lastly, being a recipient of an NIH grant, the laboratory became subject to pertinent regulations thereof governing the care and treatment of animals used in the research which was the subject of the grant (U.S. Dept. of Health, Education, and Welfare, Public Health Service, NIH Publication No. 80-23, Guide for the Care and Use of Laboratory Animals (rev. 1978, reprinted 1980)).

Accordingly, we do not believe the legislature intended section 59 of Article 27 to apply to this type of research activity under a federal program. We shall, therefore, reverse Dr. Taub's conviction and remand this matter to the Circuit Court for Montgomery County with instructions to dismiss the criminal information.

In light of the above, State's motion to strike is denied.

SENATE—ASSEMBLY

March 6, 1984

IN SENATE -- Introduced by Sens. KEHOE, BRUNO, DALY, FARLEY, GOODHUE, PADAVAN, TRUNZO, TULLY -- read twice and ordered printed, and when printed to be committed to the Committee on Agriculture

IN ASSEMBLY -- Introduced by M. of A. ROBACH, HOYT -- Multi-Sponsored by -- M. of A. BIANCHI, CONNERS, CONNOR, COOKE, D'ANDREA, DAVIS, Del TORO, DUGAN, ENGEL, FELDMAN, FLANAGAN, GOTTFRIED, GRABER, GRANNIS, HARENBERG, HARRISON, HEALEY, HEVESI, HINCHEY, HOBLOCK, HOCHBRUECKNER, JACOBS, KOPPELL, LASHER, LEVY, LIPSCHUTZ, MADISON, MARCHISELLI, MAYER-SOHN, NADLER, NAGLE, NEWBURGER, PERONE, PROUD, RUGGIERO, A. W. RYAN, SANDERS, SEMINERIO, SHEFFER II, SIEGEL, SLAUGHTER, WALDON, WALSH, WEINSTEIN, WEPRIN, WILSON, YEVOLI, YOUNG -- read once and referred to the Committee on Agriculture

AN ACT to amend the agriculture and markets law, in relation to criminal penalties for animal fighting and repealing certain provisions of such law relating thereto

The People of the State of New York, represented in Senate and Assembly, do enact as follows:

Section 1. Sections three hundred fifty-one and three hundred fifty-two of the agriculture and markets law are REPEALED and a new section three hundred fifty-one is added to read as follows:
§ 351. Prohibition of animal fighting. 1. For purposes of this section, the term "animal fighting" shall mean any fight between cocks or other birds, or between dogs, bulls, bears or any other animals, or between any such animal and a person or persons, except in exhibitions of a kind commonly featured at rodeos.
2. Any person who engages in any of the following conduct is guilty of a felony and is punishable by imprisonment for a period not to exceed four years, or by a fine not to exceed twenty-five thousand dollars, or by both such fine and imprisonment:
(a) For amusement or gain, causes any animal to engage in animal fighting; or
(b) Trains any animal under circumstances evincing an intent that such animal engage in animal fighting for amusement or gain; or

EXPLANATION--Matter in *italics* (underscored) is new; matter in brackets [ ] is old law to be omitted.

LBD15825-02-4

(c) Permits any act described in paragraph (a) or (b) of this subdivision to occur on premises under his control; or

(d) Owns, possesses or keeps any animal trained to engage in animal fighting on premises where an exhibition of animal fighting is being conducted under circumstances evincing an intent that such animal engage in animal fighting.

3. (a) Any person who engages in conduct specified in paragraph (b) of this subdivision is guilty of a misdemeanor and is punishable by imprisonment for a period not to exceed one year, or by a fine not to exceed fifteen thousand dollars, or by both such fine and imprisonment.

(b) The owning, possessing or keeping of any animal under circumstances evincing an intent that such animal engage in animal fighting.

4. (a) Any person who engages in conduct specified in paragraph (b) hereof is guilty of a misdemeanor and is punishable by imprisonment for a period not to exceed one year, or by a fine not to exceed one thousand dollars, or by both such fine and imprisonment.

(b) The knowing presence as a spectator having paid an admission fee or having made a wager at any place where an exhibition of animal fighting is being conducted.

§ 2. This act shall take effect on the first day of November next succeeding the date on which it shall have become a law.

Appendix J
Suggestions for Further Reading

CRUELTY

Dichter, "Legal Definitions of Cruelty and Animal Rights," Boston College Environmental Affairs Law Review 147 (1978)

Friend, "Animal Cruelty Laws: The Case for Reform." 8 University of Richmond Law Review 201 (1974).

LABORATORY ANIMALS

Rikleen, "The Animal Welfare Act: Still a Cruelty to Animals," 7 Boston College Environmental Affairs Law Review 129 (1978).

Singer, Animal Liberation; Avon books, 1977.

WILDLIFE

Amory, Man Kind? Dell books, 1974.

Coggins, "Federal Wildlife Law Achieves Adolescence: Developments in the 1970's," 1978 Duke Law Journal 753 (1978).

Coggins, "Wildlife and the Constitution: The Walls Came Tumbling Down," 55 Washington Law Review 295 (1980).

Coggins and Smith, "The Emerging Law of

Wildlife: A Narrative Bibliography,"   6
Environmental Law 383 (1976).

Coggins and Ward, "The Law of Wildlife
Management on the Federal Public Lands," 60
Oregon Law Review 59 (1981).

"The Emerging Law of Wildlife II: A Narrative
Bibliography of Federal Wildlife Law," 4 Harvard
Environmental Law Review (1980).

ENDANGERED SPECIES ACT

Erdheim, "The Wake of the Snail Darter:
Insuring the Effectiveness of Section 7 of the
Endangered Species Act," 9 Ecology Law
Quarterly 629 (1981).

Ganong, "Endangered Species Act Amendments
of 1978: A Congressional Response to Tennessee
Valley Authority v. Hill," 5 Columbia Journal of
Environmental Law 283 (1979).

Goplerud, "The Endangered Species Act: Does It
Jeopardize the Continued Existence of Species?"
1979 Arizona State Law Journal 487 (1979).

Harrington, "The Endangered Species Act and
the Search for Balance," 21 Natural Resources
Journal 71 (1981).

Lachenmeier, "The Endangered Species Act of
1973:   Preservation   or   Pandemonium?"   5
Environmental Law 29 (1974).

Liner, "Environmental Law - The Endangered Species Act of 1979: Congress Responds to Tennessee Valley Authority v. Hill," 25 Wayne Law Review 1327 (1979).

Sagoff, "On the Preservation of Species," 7 Columbia Journal of Environmental Law 33 (1980).

MARINE MAMMALS

Coggins, "Legal Protection for Marine Mammals: An Overview of Innovative Resources Conservation Legislation," 6 Environmental Law 1 (1975).

Herrington and Regenstein, "The Plight of Ocean Mammals," 1 Environmental Affairs 792 (1971).

Hyde, "Dolphin Conservation in the Tuna Industry: The United States' Role in an International Problem," 16 San Diego Law Review 665 (1979).

Rich, "The Tuna-Porpoise Controversy," 1 Harvard Environmental Law Review 142 (1976).

Travalio and Clement, "International Protection of Marine Mammals," 5 Columbia Journal of Environmental Law 199 (1979).

HORSES AND BURROS

Santini, "Good Intentions Gone "Estray" - The

Wild Free-Roaming Horse and Burro Act," 16 Land and Water Review 525 (1981).

Johnston, "The Fight to Save a Memory," 50 Texas Law Review 1055 (1972). [The Wild Free-Roaming Horse and Burro Act.]

MIGRATORY BIRDS

Margolin, "Liability Under the Migratory Bird Treaty Act," 7 Ecology Law Quarterly 989 (1979).

INDEX

147